Stop and rest for a minute. Then try again, with the opposite arm raised this time. Again, record your observations.

Suggested timings are given for each activity. These are only a guide. You may like to note how long it took you to complete this activity, as it may help in planning the time needed for working through the sessions.

Time taken on activity

Time management is important. While we recognise that people learn at different speeds, this pack is designed to take 20 study hours (your tutor will also advise you). You should allocate time during each week for study.

Take some time now to identify likely periods that you can set aside for study during the week.

	Mon	Tues	Wed	Thurs	Fri	Sat	Sun
am							
pm							
eve							

At the end of the learning pack, there is a learning review to help you assess whether you have achieved the learning objectives.

PSYCHOLOGICAL ASPECTS OF CARING
in a mixed economy

Martin Caraher MSc (HEd) Dip H Ed Dip Env Health

Principal Lecturer in Health Promotion, Wolfson School of Health Sciences,
Thames Valley University, London

Di Marks-Maran BSc RGN RNT DipN (London)

Resource Based Learning Manager, Wolfson School of Health Sciences,
Thames Valley University, London

THE OPEN LEARNING FOUNDATION

CHURCHILL LIVINGSTONE

NEW YORK EDINBURGH LONDON MADRID MELBOURNE SAN FRANCISCO AND TOKYO 1997

CHURCHILL LIVINGSTONE
Medical Division of Longman Group UK Limited

Distributed in the United States of America by Churchill
Livingstone Inc., 650 Avenue of the Americas, New York,
N.Y. 10011, and by associated companies, branches and
representatives throughout the world.

First published 1997

ISBN 0 443 05733 8

British Library of Cataloguing in Publication Data
A catalogue record for this book is available from the
British Library.

Library of Congress Cataloging in Publication Data
A catalog record for this book is available from the
Library of Congress

Produced through Longman Malaysia, PP

For The Open Learning Foundation

Director of Programmes: Leslie Mapp
Series Editor: Peter Birchenall
Programmes Manager: Kathleen Farren
Production Manager: Steve Moulds

For Churchill Livingstone

Director (Nursing and Allied Health): Peter Shepherd
Project Controller: Derek Robertson
Project Manager: Valerie Burgess
Design Direction: Judith Wright
Sales Promotion Executive: Maria O'Connor

CONTENTS

OPEN LEARNING FOUNDATION TEAM MEMBERS

Writer: Martin Caraher
Principal Lecturer in Health Promotion, Wolfson School of
Health Sciences,
Thames Valley University, London

Di Marks-Maran
Resource Based Learning Manager, Wolfson School of Health Sciences,
Thames Valley University, London

Editor: Lesley Partridge

Reviewers: Ann Wakefield
Nurse Tutor, School of Nursing and Midwifery,
University College Chester

Denis Turner
Nurse Tutor, School of Nursing and Midwifery,
University College Chester

Series Editor: Peter Birchenall
OLF Programme Head,
Health and Nursing,
University of Humberside

THE OPEN LEARNING FOUNDATION

Higher education has grown considerably in recent years. As well as catering for more students, universities are facing the challenge of providing for an increasingly diverse student population. Students have a wider range of backgrounds and previous educational qualifications. There are greater numbers of mature students. There is a greater need for part-time courses and continuing education and professional development programmes.

The Open Learning Foundation helps over 20 member institutions meet this growing and diverse demand – through the production of high-quality teaching and learning materials, within a strategy of creating a framework for more flexible learning. It offers member institutions the capability to increase their range of teaching options and to cover subjects in greater breadth and depth.

It does not enrol its own students. Rather, The Open Learning Foundation, by developing and promoting the greater use of open and distance learning, enables universities and others in higher education to make study more accessible and cost-effective for individual students and for business through offering more choice and more flexible courses.

Formed in 1990, the Foundation's policy objectives are to:

- improve the quality of higher education and training

- increase the quantity of higher education and training

- raise the efficiency of higher education and training delivery.

In working to meet these objectives, The Open Learning Foundation develops new teaching and learning materials, encourages and facilitates more and better staff development, and promotes greater responsiveness to change within higher education institutions. The Foundation works in partnership with its members and other higher education bodies to develop new approaches to teaching and learning.

In developing new teaching and learning materials, the Foundation has:

- a track record of offering customers a swift and flexible response

- a national network of members able to provide local support and guidance

- the ability to draw on significant national expertise in producing and delivering open learning

- complete freedom to seek out the best writers, materials and resources to secure development.

Other titles in this series

INTRODUCTION

Welcome to this open learning unit, *Psychological Aspects of Caring in a Mixed Economy*. This unit is designed to help you explore the psychological aspects of caring in the changing society we live in. We will explore the term 'mixed economy' in greater detail later; for the moment it is sufficient to say that this means the provision of care by statutory services (such as health and local authorities), the private sector and voluntary groups.

A definition of psychology which we like and which encompasses what we are trying to achieve in this unit comes from Ornstein and Carresten (1991):

'**Psychology** is a complete science of human experience and behaviour'.

This encompasses three dimensions: experience, behaviour and the interaction between these two. The focus of this unit is on the interaction between experiences and behaviour and making sense of them in the context of care and caring. There are lots of psychology textbooks but very few deal with 'caring'. This unit applies psychological theory and principles to the roles and behaviours involved in caring.

Another useful definition of psychology is:'the scientific study of behaviour and mental processes.'

You do not need to have a psychology background to work through this unit, but we recommend you have a psychology textbook or a psychology dictionary handy for reference. A list is given in further reading.

Generally, there are two approaches to psychology as a subject of study. In the first, psychological aspects and traits are viewed as being inherent in the person and result in interactions with the outside environment. This is the root of the 'nature argument'. Within this view, psychological traits are inherited.

The second approach to psychology is known as social psychology. This recognises the interaction between the individual and the environment in the shaping of psychological attributes and behaviours.

We use both approaches, but it is fair to say that the unit mirrors more of the second approach.

The issues of caring are examined from two viewpoints:

intrinsic – the impact of the caring role on the psychology of the individual

extrinsic – the impact of the individual and group psychology on roles and relationships.

We present a number of models to facilitate and make sense of the concepts. You do not have to agree with the models but you should be able to understand the working and logic behind them. We have devised the models in Sessions Three and Seven to help you make sense of the concepts and principles. They are not necessarily applicable to real-life situations.

The unit is designed to stand on its own, but it has a companion unit *The Social Context of Caring in a Mixed Economy*. You can study either unit first. The unit consists of seven sessions which build on one another.

Session One explores the historical development of caring.

Session Two looks at what we mean by caring and explores the different types of caring.

Session Three begins to assemble the issues raised in the first two sessions to look at the psychology of care. This is then followed by the scrutiny of the role of carers from a psychological perspective.

The first two sessions put the issue of caring into context. It is from Session Three onwards that a psychology of care is assembled and examined. **Sessions Four, Five and Six** examine various aspects of caring roles and groups and support for carers.

Session Seven brings the whole unit together. It looks at the conditions which contribute to a healthy caring relationship. We use a model specially devised for this unit to do this.

LEARNING PROFILE

Given below is a list of learning outcomes for each session of this unit. You can use it to identify your current learning and so to consider how this unit can help you to develop your knowledge and understanding. The list is not intended to cover all of the details discussed in every session, and so the learning profile should only be used for general guidance.

For each of the learning outcomes listed below, tick the box that corresponds most closely to the point you feel you are at now. This will provide you with an assessment of your current understanding and confidence in the areas you will study in this unit.

	Not at all	Partly	Quite well	Very well

Session One

I can:
- give examples of different forms of caring   □   □   □   □
- discuss what constitutes quality care   □   □   □   □
- distinguish between the different categories of care   □   □   □   □
- begin to recognise aspects of psychology and how these relate to providing care.   □   □   □   □

Session Two

I can:
- give examples of changes in care   □   □   □   □
- relate improvements in the physical and social environment to changing ways of providing care   □   □   □   □

	Not at all	Partly	Quite well	Very well

Session Two *continued*

- critically discuss some of the myths underlying the provision of care in the community □ □ □ □
- give examples of the various organisations which make up the voluntary, independent and statutory sectors □ □ □ □
- critically examine and provide reasons for the growth of the informal sector □ □ □ □
- explain how social pressures influence carers and their behaviour. □ □ □ □

Session Three

I can:

- critically examine and give examples of factors that influence the psychology of the carer □ □ □ □
- critically examine and give examples of factors that influence the psychology of the caring role □ □ □ □
- critically examine and give examples of factors that influence the responsibilities of the carer □ □ □ □
- discuss and give examples of interactions between these three elements. □ □ □ □

Session Four

I can:

- critically examine and give examples of role development and role casting □ □ □ □
- give examples of the usefulness of roles in the caring relationship □ □ □ □
- critically examine the positive and negative strokes and feedback that carers receive □ □ □ □
- give examples of the negative aspects of role casting or occupation in formal and informal care settings □ □ □ □
- discuss critically the interrelationships between various roles in the caring situation □ □ □ □

	Not at all	Partly	Quite well	Very well

Session Four *continued*

- critically examine role relationships between formal and informal carers

| | ☐ | ☐ | ☐ | ☐ |

- reflect on the problems in role relationship between formal and informal carers and conflicts with regard to who the client is.

| | ☐ | ☐ | ☐ | ☐ |

Session Five

I can:

- identify who informal carers are and critically analyse what kinds of care they give

| | ☐ | ☐ | ☐ | ☐ |

- describe the psychological impact of being an informal carer

| | ☐ | ☐ | ☐ | ☐ |

- describe the kind of psychological support which informal carers may require

| | ☐ | ☐ | ☐ | ☐ |

- give examples of approaches to informal care networks and groups and critically examine the impact these networks have on the psychology of the carer.

| | ☐ | ☐ | ☐ | ☐ |

Session Six

I can:

- critically examine the role of individuals in shaping group philosophy

| | ☐ | ☐ | ☐ | ☐ |

- give examples of the range of activities voluntary groups provide

| | ☐ | ☐ | ☐ | ☐ |

- discuss the implications of the psychological contract for individuals and groups

| | ☐ | ☐ | ☐ | ☐ |

- identify and critically examine the needs which voluntary groups meet for their members

| | ☐ | ☐ | ☐ | ☐ |

- critically explore the impact of the mixed economy of care on the voluntary sector.

| | ☐ | ☐ | ☐ | ☐ |

Session Seven

I can:

- define and discuss in depth what is meant by a healthy caring relationship

| | ☐ | ☐ | ☐ | ☐ |

	Not at all	Partly	Quite well	Very well

Session Seven *continued*

- use an interactionist model to critically explore caring relationships $\square$ $\square$ $\square$ $\square$

- discuss the conditions within the interactionist model which enable a caring relationship to be a healthy one $\square$ $\square$ $\square$ $\square$

- identify ways in which agencies and organisations within the mixed economy of care can contribute to healthy caring relationships. $\square$ $\square$ $\square$ $\square$

SESSION ONE

What is caring?

Introduction

In the introduction to this unit we gave some guidance on how to work through the sessions. To summarise, you should:

- use short periods of study

- do the activities; don't just skip to the commentary

- review your learning in small sections before moving on

- think critically: you are not expected to agree with everything presented but you should understand it.

The purpose of this session is to begin to examine some of the component parts of care so that we can use them as building blocks for the other sessions.

When we talk of carers the images conjured up in most people's minds are of family, relatives, friends and of caring at home. The word 'carer' has connotations which go beyond the formal provision of practical care but which also suggest the involvement of emotional and psychological elements. What is involved for those giving care, why they do it, the psychological benefits and costs of caring, are important questions to consider.

The current emphasis on community care or care in the community is a retreat from institutional care. This session explores what we mean by care and explains the origins and philosophy of this shift in caring. We will begin by examining issues related to care within what are considered to be 'normal' situations and then explore what is considered outside the 'norm' of what is expected of carers.

Session objectives

When you have completed this session you should be able to:

- give examples of different forms of caring

- identify the rewards and frustrations associated with informal and formal caring

- discuss 'care with a smile' or what constitutes quality care

- distinguish between the different categories of care

- begin to recognise aspects of psychology and how these relate to providing care.

1: What is caring?

Caring at its simplest is looking after people. This includes a broad range of activities and events. You can provide care for people who can care for themselves but who choose not to, for those who need permanent care and for those who require care for intermittent or particular periods of time.

Some commentators (such as Aggleton (1990)) discuss health in terms of physical, mental and social health. Similarly, these three elements provide a framework for care i.e.:

- physical care

- emotional care

- social care.

The provision of care is something that is determined not just by the needs of particular individuals or groups but also by what is socially appropriate.

ACTIVITY I   ALLOW **15** MINUTES

Think of children's development and their needs, starting from birth to 15 years. Think particularly of the differences in care they may require and receive at different stages and include physical, emotional and social care needs and care requirements.

The chart below is divided into three sections, from birth to 5 years old, from 6 to 12 years old and from 13 to 15 years old. List the types of care children receive as they grow older. Use the headings to help you identify different aspects of care.

Type of care			
	Physical	**Emotional**	**Social**
Birth to 5 years			
6 to 12 years			
13 to 15 years			

Commentary

You may have identified that babies and young children need lots of physical attention and caring for. Babies need to be clothed, fed and bathed. They need looking after in a very physical way. In addition they need emotional care and support, which in the early stages is not separate from the physical care provided. Socialisation into culturally acceptable behaviour patterns begins early in life. Parental role modelling of 'good' as opposed to 'bad' behaviour will influence a child when responding to others and provide the building blocks for moral and social health.

When children go to playschool or primary school, the care they receive changes in its nature. It becomes a mixture of physical and emotional care. The emotional care is given verbally and non-verbally. Care changes from being the concern of the family to also being the concern of non-family carers such as teachers.

As children move into adolescence, their need for independence and the formation of self-identity mean that the care provided becomes much more indirect. This is partly because adolescence is a transition period where individuals move from being 'cared for' to caring for themselves. It is also due to social mores and the association of adolescence with emerging sexuality. For example, it becomes less appropriate and acceptable in western culture to touch adolescents. So the care provided for adolescents changes from 'caring for' to 'caring about' them.

This notion of 'caring for' has strong associations of hands-on care. In the early stages of life, such 'caring for' is how babies receive most of their psychological stimulation. As children grow and become more self-reliant, the care given changes from hands-on care to 'caring about'. This includes giving children both verbal and non-verbal communication about their behaviour and actions. It may mean providing direction and setting limits for children. It is also about getting them ready for adult life.

Social care is often provided by the state and by legislation which is intended to protect children. In the period from '0 to 5' social care is provided by midwives, health visitors, GPs and social services. Voluntary groups, such as playgroups, and institutions like schools provide another range of services in the ages from '6 to 12' and between ages '13 to 15'. The change in the social care provided over this later period is moving from 'caring for' children to preparing them for independence.

Individuals may require physical, emotional and social care. For the moment we will focus on the physical aspect of caring. It is important to remember that the provision of physical care can communicate other elements of care. For example, handling someone 'roughly' or without due concern for their feelings communicates messages of not caring in an emotional or psychological sense for the individual.

ACTIVITY 2
ALLOW 15 MINUTES

Can you think of carers who are allowed to break social mores and engage in physical contact with adolescents? You may find it helpful to consider particular circumstances, as this may make it easier to identify the groups of people.

Write your ideas here.

Commentary

You may have come up with a list which includes doctors, nurses, dentists and in certain circumstances parents and other members of the family. These people fall into the category of carers. The situations you have considered may have included times of illness, pain and uncertainty, when adolescents revert to needing to be 'cared for'. Being cared for is a form of reassurance.

Taking on the role of carer allows you to do things which in other circumstances might be deemed inappropriate. It may also allow you access to information which in other instances might be inappropriate. The idea that caring has a formal role is one which we will explore in Session Three. For the moment it is enough to recognise that those who take on caring roles are allowed certain dispensations in terms of their behaviour towards those receiving the care.

It may also be that over our life span we start out by requiring lots of physical care and end up needing it. The period in between is for most of us a time when we seek out emotional and loving care. As we have already suggested, physical care – for example, how you touch someone – can also communicate feelings of care.

2: Who are the carers?

So far, we have seen that there are different types of care. There are also different types of carer: those who provide care because of some sense of love and duty and those who provide care because they are trained and paid to do so. The people in these two categories are often crudely termed informal and formal carers. Many informal carers perform a role which society expects. Looking after children is a role that many women want or expect to fulfil as a mother.

The traditional role of women as carers is often extended to the expectation that women will change their lives to care. This works from two perspectives:

- external expectations and demands on women on how to be carers

- internal perception by women themselves that they will provide care.

This is a chicken and egg situation with the internal and external expectations reproducing one another. As the SCOPE (1995) report notes:

> 'This is not to say that respondents [women] would choose not to care, rather that their choices are constrained by the norms of the society in which we live'.
> (SCOPE, 1995, p2)

Caring is a role carried out by females across their life span. Women as mothers take on the greater burden of care for children. In the middle and/or later years of the life span, women are more likely to end up providing care, perhaps for siblings, parents or even parents-in-law.

Women's work is often called 'hidden'. The caring role is carried out behind closed doors and is not open to public view. Women are also expected to cope without seeking help, as caring is seen as an expected part of a woman's role in society. The above quote from SCOPE highlights the problem that carers are not helped in their role by society, or by the expectation that they will cope. This is particularly true of women in the caring role.

The division between formal and informal carers leads to a system of well-defined activities performed by the two groups. One example of this is the failure to include informal carers in the process of assessment (DOH, 1995). Assessment is seen as a process which can only be carried out by professional or formal carers. They are trained to determine needs. Assessment is not viewed as a partnership or co-operative process but as one requiring professional input.

ACTIVITY 3 — ALLOW 20 MINUTES

The recognition given to formal or professional carers and informal carers differs. You may like to look through the local and national papers to see what type of care-giving is reported favourably. Think of different forms of **recognition** and **reward** for different types of caring. Make a list under the headings of formal and informal carers.

	Rewards from providing care	Recognition from providing care
Formal carers		
Informal carers		

'Recognition': *is related to carers receiving due regard for professionalism, personal sacrifice and selflessness when performing their work.* 'Reward' *is related to financial payment or feelings of personal satisfaction resulting from the caring activity.*

Commentary

Formal carers are rewarded by being paid for their work. Their role, whether they are district nurses, social workers or care managers, receives social recognition in the general acknowledgement of a job worth doing. They are often given official recognition by the training or professional qualifications required to carry out their role. The gratitude of clients is another reward as well as recognition.

Informal carers on the other hand carry out a role which is hidden from public view. They don't wear a uniform which equates to a role and the caring takes place in their own home. Informal carers could include a mother looking after a toddler, a family caring for their teenager with Down's syndrome or a husband caring for his wife with senile dementia. Such roles are often not recognised or officially rewarded. They are carried out as a result of duty and love. Informal carers gain reward and recognition from the physical act of caring and from the thought of a job well done (Grant and Nolan, 1993). This aspect of informal care is often ignored in the research literature. Despite frustrations and problems with caring, many informal carers choose to care for a relative or friend. The frustrations arise from a lack of support and a lack of social recognition for their role.

The rewards informal carers receive need to be balanced with the frustrations many face in not being recognised, and in carrying out a full-time job with no financial remuneration. A major criticism of carers' allowances is that they are meant to relieve informal carers from other demands and leave them free to provide care. This is not the same as rewarding them for their labours and leads to a lack of recognition of their role and a loss of self-esteem and motivation. (Twigg, 1992)

Many carers have to give up paid work to care. This obviously means a loss in income but there is also a loss of self-worth which is exaggerated by two issues:

● dependence on benefits

● the low social value publicly given to being a carer.

As the SCOPE report states:

> 'many organisations will not accept 'carer' as an occupation. This can lead to difficulties, for example with obtaining credit or insurance cover. I was recently advised by a credit company to describe myself as 'self-employed' in order that my application might be accepted'.
> (SCOPE, 1995)

Carers are angered by the lack of recognition they receive from the government and society. They suffer financial hardship. The following quote from a SCOPE report highlights this:

> 'The people who hold the budgets should realise how much unpaid carers save the community financially – not how much the disabled person is costing the services. Care in the community in the government's eyes is the answer to everything, when in fact it's the cheap option'.
> (SCOPE, 1995)

Many surveys have found that the work carried out by informal carers does not significantly differ from that provided by formal carers. The monetary allowance that informal carers receive does not reflect this (Atkin, 1992).

ACTIVITY 4   ALLOW 15 MINUTES

Can you think of any reasons why informal carers' allowances do not equate with the pay of formal carers? Write your suggestions down.

Commentary

Among the reasons you may have come up with are the ideas that informal care is cheap care and that informal care is considered to be a duty or labour of love that should be performed without payment. This is similar to the argument about payment of families for child care. Many feminists argue that women as the main carers of children perform a function that the state refuses to recognise.

A recent report from SCOPE (1995) estimated the hidden costs of caring as being in the order of £34 billion a year. This was estimated on the basis of the cost to the state if these services had to be provided by formal carers.

Another argument is that informal care is menial work which does not require formal training or skills. We will explore this in more detail later in the unit.

Society expects that families, and women in particular, should provide care. This association of care with women's work makes care a gender issue. The fact that the care occurs in the home and not in an institutional setting further undermines its claim to being valid work.

3: The meanings within formal and informal care

The use of the words informal and formal carers suggests a hierarchy of services, some of which are more important than others. Formal care is delivered by trained, professional and paid staff. So informal care may be thought to be of lower quality and provided by untrained individuals.

The word informal is also used in the sense of the relationship between the carer and the person receiving the care. Many informal carers are related to the individual for whom they care. This caring relationship is not just about providing care but is complicated by all sorts of other aspects of the relationship and personal agendas. Informal care often occurs in the context of 'family or marital relationships and is on an unpaid basis that draws on feelings of love, obligation and duty' (Twigg, 1992, p.2).

It is easier for professionals to establish formal relationships based on their caring role as professionals rather than on personal issues. The basis for their relationship is their occupation.

Informal care provided by families – especially women – is strongly linked to a romanticised view of the past where care is provided within loving and caring families. We will explore the notion that care is traditionally family-based in the next session.

We use the terms informal care and informal carers throughout the unit to describe the relationship carers have with those receiving the care. The terms informal care and informal carer are not used to suggest that the services provided are of a lesser value or inferior to those offered by formal carers (Atkin, 1992).

ACTIVITY 5   ALLOW 30 MINUTES

Think of your family and/or circle of friends. Make a list of those receiving informal care in your family or among your circle of friends. Identify the sources of any informal care (no matter how informal). Also make a list of support services (again these may be informal) which carers receive.

Use a domainal map to do this. In a domainal map you locate yourself in the middle of the page and place those nearest you (i.e. in terms of relationships) closest to you on the domainal map and those who do not have a close relationship with you further away from you on the domainal map.

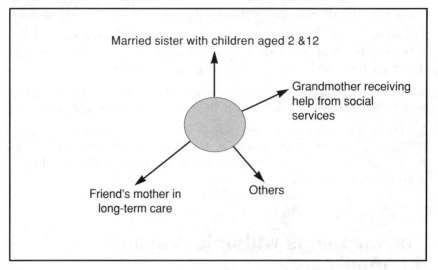

Figure 1: Example of a domainal map

Now draw your own domainal map.

Commentary

You will probably have found a range of caring activities, from mothers with children to friends/relatives caring for elderly relatives. You may be able to agree with these generalisations:

- most carers are women

- care occurs within family relationships

- most care is provided for the very young and the very old

- the range of formal support and care services is limited

- most care occurs within family settings although this is not equally distributed amongst family members.

The other issue that may have arisen is that some informal carers work for organisations as volunteers. While a majority of informal carers are family or neighbours, some contribute their time and energy as volunteers. Local carers' groups are volunteers who do things like shopping, sitting and gardening. What this group of carers has in common with family carers is that they are often unpaid, untrained volunteers, whose work is hidden from public view.

4: What is reasonable? – the scope of the informal carer

We have looked at situations which fit into the 'norm' of looking after children or providing care to those who are sick or frail. What is expected of us as carers is dictated by society's values. The expectation is that children will grow up and gradually wean themselves off the family and go off to set up their own family units. There are situations where this does not happen.

ACTIVITY 6   ALLOW 15 MINUTES

Can you think of two examples of 'physical' and 'psychological' conditions which would inhibit the ability of children to become independent after adolescence? Note them down.

Beside each example note down the rewards and satisfactions as well as the frustrations the carers may face.

Commentary

Although there are no hard and fast rules, there are circumstances which make it harder for adults to establish their independence. Some examples of physical conditions are:

- confined to wheelchair
- cystic fibrosis
- cerebral palsy.

Some psychological (or mental health) conditions are:

- Down syndrome
- schizophrenia
- severe depression.

None of these conditions necessarily means that people can't live independent lives, but rather that independent living is harder and less likely to occur without the help of informal or formal carers. It is important not to confuse a physical or psychological condition with the inability to achieve independence. People in wheelchairs say that the block to independent living is not the wheelchair but the sixteen steps leading to the building.

What happens to children who may never achieve independence? The onus is on informal carers to continue to provide care for family members or relatives. This imposes a sense of responsibility and duty on the carer which is sometimes referred to as **ultra obligation**.

Ultra obligation goes beyond the 'normal' expectation of caring which is raising children to a stage where they are psychologically and physically independent. While many families would wish to provide care for a parent, son, daughter, spouse or loved one if they need it , it is important to recognise the psychological strain which ultra obligation imposes on informal carers.

Ultra obligation:
'Committing one's life to caring for another person'.

The question arises: how much do we as members of society expect informal carers to devote their lives to providing care? In other words, what is reasonable? This becomes a moral issue. Read the next activity and reflect on the questions.

ACTIVITY 7 · ALLOW 20 MINUTES

Read Case Study 1 and answer the questions at the end.

CASE STUDY 1

Jimmy is a 12-year-old who attends his local secondary school. He is bright and attentive while at school. He gets on well with his classmates but has no close friends. Recently he has not been doing his homework and appears tired.

He lives with his mother in a small two-bedroom flat which is rented. His parents are divorced and he rarely sees his father, who lives 60 miles away. Jimmy's mother is suffering from depression. For periods of time she functions normally, then for no apparent reason becomes sullen and withdrawn. She rarely leaves the flat but just sits there smoking, with the TV on, although she is not watching it.

During these periods, Jimmy has to do all the housework and the shopping; he has to pay the bills and generally look after his mother. He is afraid that if he complains or tells anyone he will be taken away from his mother and put in a home. He rarely brings friends home or talks to anyone about the problem.

Do you think Jimmy is performing a role that falls within the scope of what we would consider 'normal'? Note some of the effects the situation is having on his behaviour and how it may be affecting his psychological health.

Commentary

It is often hard to separate out normal help from extra demands. The Health Services Management Unit in a study of young carers (1995) says that they 'struggle to cope and care and are often unwilling to admit problems'.

Most people would consider Jimmy's role to be burdensome, in that he takes on extra responsibilities. His behaviour is affected in that he carries out all the physical tasks around the house and seems constantly tired. These additional responsibilities are more than would be expected of a 12-year-old. The psychological burden includes worrying about his mother and what will happen to the family unit, having no one to talk to and feeling fear and pressure at school because of his inability to do homework.

Children with disabled parents often bear such burdens (Health Service Management Unit, 1995). The burdens of this additional care are often hidden and little is done to relieve them. When it appears to the outside world that a person is coping, it is his or her informal carer, in this case the child, who is bearing an additional burden. This may not be acknowledged. Children as carers will be considered further in Session Five.

Atkin (1992) sets out six different forms of caring relationship which affect the experience of care and the functions carers carry out. These six forms of caring are:

- spouse carers

- parental carers

- filial carers

- sibling carers

- child carers

- non-kin carers.

There is a gender bias running through all these six forms of care. Women are more likely to fill the caring role, whether as a spouse, parent, sibling, filial child or non-kin carer. There is also evidence that daughters-in-law are more likely to act as carers than are sons (Atkin, 1992).

5: Care with a smile?

Care is not just about giving or receiving good technical or physical care. It is also about the way this care is delivered. The issues of quality of care are often concerned with the psychological delivery of care. In the business and commercial sectors it is not considered sufficient just to deliver goods or services efficiently. The manner in which service is delivered is equally important. Work through the activity below for an example of this.

ACTIVITY 8   ALLOW 15 MINUTES

Think about the last time you received services you were unhappy with, perhaps in a restaurant, a shop or a visit to the cinema. Sketch out the sequence of events and identify what made you unhappy or dissatisfied.

Commentary

Some examples of dissatisfaction you may have identified are: having to wait too long, bad service or shoddy goods. But the behaviour of the person serving you will probably have had a large impact on your lack of satisfaction. Services or goods delivered with a poor attitude are not valued as highly as those delivered with a smile or in a pleasant way. Similarly, care which is just technically good may not necessarily be well received.

Informal carers may find it difficult to deliver care with a smile as they receive little reward or acknowledgement and may even be giving care to someone who is not fully aware of what is happening. Escape may not be an option for informal carers, and this imposes an additional psychological strain.

The involvement of formal carers with the person being cared for is not as intense, and it is easier to deliver care with a smile when you know you can walk away from the situation. Professional carers or volunteers may wish to keep some distance between themselves and the client. The relationship may be defined in terms of the functions the formal carer is there to perform. So, for example, the district nurse may be concerned primarily about the physical effects of the patient's medicine, the home help about general care and safety in the house.

Such boundaries in relationships are less clearly defined for informal carers. Here the caring relationship is complicated by family relationships, so it can be harder for informal carers to establish a distance which may offer some protection to their individual psyche.

6: Categories of care

We have distinguished between caring for and caring about, begun to make some distinctions between different types of carers, looked at differences between formal and informal carers and begun to examine what constitutes 'normal' care. Now we turn to different categories of care. These are:

1   personal care

2   domestic care

3   auxiliary care

4   social care or support and

5   surveillance.

These categories of care often merge and individual carers may perform more than one type. The list nonetheless helps us make sense of the range of care.

ACTIVITY 9   ALLOW 25 MINUTES

Look at the categories of care given above. For each category consider:

● what this care may involve

● who might provide it

● what psychological benefits the carer would receive.

Write your comments in the chart below.

You may find it useful to base your comments on a particular example of someone requiring care, for example, someone who has AIDS.

	Give examples of what this entails	Who might provide this care?	What psychological benefits would the carer receive?
Personal care			
Domestic care			
Auxiliary care			
Social care or support			
Surveillance			

Commentary

An outline of the type of care required by someone who has AIDS and who is living with his partner appears in *Table 1*.

	Examples	Provided by	Psychological benefits to carer
Personal care	Bathing	Partner within a loving and caring relationship	Providing support
	Administering drugs, dressings and toiletting	District nurse	Maintaining the client at an optimum level of health and well being
Domestic care	Cooking and cleaning	Partner Home help	Maintaining a safe, clean and supportive environment
Auxiliary care	Taking to doctor or visit to shops Sitting services	Neighbour or friends Volunteers	Feeling of having helped/contributed as a member of the caring team
Social support	Visits	Volunteers or friends	Feeling of empathy
Surveillance	keep an eye on things during the day	Neighbour or friends	Being part of a caring and supportive community. Engenders a spirit of empathy and a sense of being useful.

Table 1: Types of care (a patient with AIDS)

The different types of care demand different commitments and skills. This is important in terms of the willingness of people to provide the level of care needed. A neighbour may be happy to provide surveillance for an elderly person by keeping an eye on whether curtains are pulled or milk taken in from the doorstep, but the same neighbour may not wish to provide domestic or personal care services. On the other hand we expect close relatives to provide personal care, often without training or any thought about how it may affect the relationship between them and the person being cared for.

The psychological benefits to the carers revolve around positive feedback and the reason why many people provide informal care. Many people carry out the activity of caring because of someone they love. Their psychological 'pay' is in the form of the feedback they receive from the person being cared for.

Summary

1 We have explored the meaning of care and what society expects of carers. The expectation is for care that fits into the 'norm'.

2 There are two general types of carers, the formal carers (people who have received professional training and education) and the informal carers who encompass a broad and diverse range of people from family members to neighbours, friends and volunteer groups.

3 Different categories of care equate with different levels of psychological and physical commitment, with each person's psychological commitment determining the type and level of care they can provide.

4 The relationship between carer and cared for is dependent on issues such as personal relationship, gender and age.

Before you move on to Session Two, check that you have achieved the objectives given at the beginning of this session and, if not, review the appropriate sections.

SESSION TWO

The roots
of care

Introduction

This session reviews the development of care in a historical and economic sense, from menial work to current trends towards community care and the mixed economy of care. By the mixed economy of care we mean the provision of services by a combination of :

- the statutory sector

- the independent sector represented by charity and voluntary groups

- the commercial or independent for-profit sector.

We rely on the past for our view of the present. So past developments play a strong part in influencing our attitudes and behaviour in providing care. Developments in care are the result of changes in ideas about treatment, the patterns of disease and social trends.

In looking at the development of care, it is important to understand:

- the myths and fallacies underlying the trend towards a mixed economy of care

- how the development towards a mixed economy of care influences the individual and group psychology of carers.

Session objectives

When you have completed this session you should be able to:

- give examples of current trends in care provision

- relate improvements in the physical and social environment to changing ways of providing care

- critically discuss some of the myths underlying the provision of care in the community

- give examples of the various organisations which make up the voluntary, independent and statutory sectors

- critically examine, and provide reasons for, the growth of the informal sector

- explain how social pressures influence carers and their behaviour.

1: Hospital care

The current trend is away from hospital care to community care (Graham, 1992). Hospitals are seen to have appropriated the role previously played by families and the community. A good place to start our historical analysis, then, is at the development of the hospital system.

ACTIVITY 10   ALLOW **10** MINUTES

Hospitals as we know them today have only developed since the mid 1800s. Take a few minutes to jot down some ideas why hospitals had not developed up until this time.

Commentary

Until the 1870s hospitals were unsafe places. Due to the lack of treatment opportunities, these were places people were sent to die. The introduction of asepsis and effective treatments began to encourage people to believe that hospitals were places where they could receive help.

Also, over 100 years ago no effective treatment existed for the common killers, infectious diseases. The increase in the population in urban areas led to more disease and illness. Hospitals provided a rudimentary level of care for those who were dying. This consisted of making people as comfortable as possible. There was little need for nurses to be trained, as there was little they could do. No effective treatment or pain relief existed. Nursing and other hospital staff performed domestic work. The nursing staff in the original hospitals were women and in most cases religious sisters (Woodham-Smith, 1991).

From charity to statutory to commercial care

The secularisation of medical and nursing care led to the development of a formal training for doctors and nurses. They moved from being informal carers – in the sense of being untrained – to formal carers.

This development also tied in with what Aston and Seymour (1990) have termed the development of therapeutic medicine. It was in this way that hospitals became the centre of healthcare offering treatment and cure.

The role of the state in the provision of services is a recent phenomenon. Before the establishment of the National Health Service in 1948, the major provider of healthcare in Britain was the voluntary sector. The state took responsibility for the provision of a public health and clinic-based system.

The establishment of the NHS brought the majority of hospitals into the state sector. The original idea was that the state, through the NHS, would wipe out all disease and illness and that there would be no use for the voluntary sector or for charities. This premise was based on two false assumptions:

- that there was a reservoir of disease and illness

- that medicine could eliminate this reservoir.

What of course happened was an epidemiological shift in the pattern of disease. Infectious diseases diminished and chronic disease increased. The realisation has been that there is no end to health needs but that there is a limit to the resources available.

Improvements in hygiene and treatment meant a decrease in the incidence of infectious diseases, but these have been replaced by what are called diseases of lifestyle such as cancers, coronary heart disease and accidents. Such 'diseases' are not infections and are not preventable from a medical viewpoint but are amenable to prevention from a position of lifestyle intervention. This has implications for the care provided.

The independent sector emerged out of this dilemma. From the mid-1960s to the present day, the number of voluntary self-help and charity groups has grown. Among the reasons for this growth are:

- lack of recognition of certain conditions

- the extension of care to include support and counselling

- the need to advocate and represent views of members/sufferers

- the need to campaign for services

- the need to campaign for changes in attitudes in society at large

- the need to represent the interests of minority groups.

The growth of the voluntary and charity sector arose out of gaps in service provision and dissatisfaction with the statutory provision. The growth of the independent, for-profit sector on the other hand, represented an attempt to economise by introducing competition to the provision of services.

ACTIVITY 11

From what you have just read, summarise the changes in the way care has been delivered since 1870.

Your summary should briefly take account of:

- improvements in medical care

- social changes and how these have affected the way that care is delivered.

Commentary

Since the 1870s there has been a shift from care provided by a domestic, menial aide to care which was defined by therapy and professional knowledge and back to care which again has its focus on domestic and menial roles. Nurses and other healthcare professionals have redefined themselves as the professional carers, supervising nursing auxiliaries and enrolled nurses in the carrying out of the menial roles. This allows them to provide the technical elements of care.

The trend towards the untrained, ill-equipped menial looking after routine tasks is not unusual. It is a feature of most professional development. Professionals do not want to provide basic menial care; their training has equipped them for what they see as more important functions. Therefore the menial functions are performed by untrained individuals. In hospitals these would be care assistants; in the community, the family or other informal carers.

Between the 1870s and today we have seen a rise and fall in the importance ascribed to hospital care. Initially hospitals were the power bases for the professions, particularly medicine and nursing. Powerful doctors and formidable matrons ruled the roost, yet as a focus for care the hospitals were, and still are, seen to be effective (Foucault, 1972). However society has witnessed profound changes in the way that primary care is delivered. The General Practice is now central to the delivery of care and has assumed an importance previously ascribed to the hospital.

The changes in care provision are summarised in *Figure 2*.

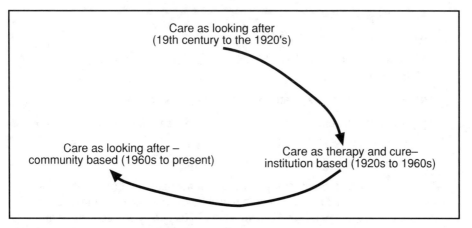

Figure 2: The three ages of care

The patterns and nature of disease and advances in technology have made it possible for care to be given in different settings. The growth of the hospice movement and hospital-at-home schemes are examples of the change in care. The hospice movement has grown out of the realisation that for terminally ill people, hospitals may not be the most appropriate places for care to be provided. Terminally ill patients require excellent technical care in terms of pain relief and medical interventions. They also require emotional and supportive care. Their families may need support. A busy ward with lots of competing demands may not be the best setting for terminally ill patients with a multitude of caring needs.

ACTIVITY 12   ALLOW 10 MINUTES

The closure of hospitals and large care institutions is occurring world-wide.

Make a list of the hospitals and institutions in your local area. Find out how many have shut in the last 20 years. You may need to ask friends, neighbours or colleagues for assistance.

Then make a second list of the possible reasons for such closures.

Commentary

You may have identified issues such as:

- the impersonal nature of hospitals
- hospitals are removed from people's everyday lives

- hospitals are too expensive

- more people are living longer

- many conditions for which people require care are not amenable to treatment or cure

- people are healthier than they were 100 years ago

- less technical care is required so 'untrained' carers can provide cheaper care than highly trained staff

- it is better to look after people in their own homes.

While there is no one reason for the closure of hospitals and other institutions, there is no doubt that the focus for care has shifted (back) to the community. The crisis of costs experienced world-wide in the 1970s and 1980s convinced many that we could not keep pumping resources into high-tech services, as their impact on health was limited.

The focus became the community. Such an approach was led by the World Health Organisation (WHO, 1985) which talked about improving communities. The idea was that resources would be shifted from large institutions to support development in the community. This is what is commonly known as community care.

2: Trends in community care: a bucolic image of the past

The move to community care has largely gone unchallenged. As Baldwin (1993) writes, many groups are now lamenting the loss of institutions and the move to non-institutional or, as it is commonly called, 'community care'.

Richard Titmuss (1968) warns that the phrase 'community care' conjures up images of 'warmth and human kindness essentially personal and comforting'. He is scathing about the idea that you could create a community where none existed before, 'let alone one that cared'.

This idea of a community that cares is, he argues, to romanticise the past. Although the notion of a bucolic or simple life unburdened by the pressures of modern living is an image commonly portrayed of Victorian times, the reality is that for many Victorians life was hard and short.

Titmuss (1968) suggests that we are trying to recreate the past in the image which suits our present. It suits us to believe that the past was good and that families were caring and supportive. It may also be an attempt to create caring communities by influencing families and individuals to perform in expected ways. In fact, past times were harsh and caring existed in a different context. There are stories of families and relatives dumping relatives in the workhouses. Sometimes this was because of the fear of infecting the rest of the family.

ACTIVITY 13   ALLOW 15 MINUTES

Can you think of reasons why care at home may not have been common in the past? Note down your ideas.

Commentary

Among the reasons you may have listed are:

- treatments didn't exist to treat people at home

- people died much younger

- people died of diseases which nowadays are treatable

- many children with disabilities would have died at birth

- poor hygiene and sanitation in the home

- extended families (see glossary) are a relatively recent phenomenon.

The following passage shows the fear people had of infection, or as it was commonly called, 'contagion'.

> A boy of 14 named James Foley... left the Killanummery hospital on 22nd January, being on a week convalescence after fever, he received from the doctor who had been in charge of the hospital, which was at that time ordered to be closed, a ticket of admission at Manorhamilton; the boy, instead of going there, returned to his father, who, fearing contagion, would not admit him among the other children, and probably from want of shelter, in addition to his weak state of health, the poor boy perished in the inclement weather or it might have been from a relapse. The father was in the receipt of out-door relief for himself and his children, including the boy James, and he did not report either his being in hospital, or his subsequent condition to the relieving officer.
> (Litton, 1994, p. 111)

The above example shows that facilities did not exist in the past to treat people at home and that the fear of contagion was justified.

Myths about the past affect the psychological pressures of caring which are placed on families today (Baldwin, 1993).

ACTIVITY 14   ALLOW 10 MINUTES

How do you think notions about caring families and individuals of the past affect carers today? Think in terms of the behaviour expected of carers and the emotions they might experience.

Write down your ideas.

Commentary

Idealised notions of caring families of the past may make individual carers feel they have to cope no matter how difficult the situation. They may feel a sense of loneliness if they are not able to admit or acknowledge problems publicly. They may be affected by emotions such as frustration, guilt, anger, despair. Some of these may be based on assumptions about what it means to be a carer. They may feel that carers are supposed to be unselfish and giving and that carers ought to cope.

It is important to understand the roots of this image. Again, we need to trace its history to understand how it affects society's expectations of carers.

3: Social expectations of carers

The development of the profession of nursing owes much to its roots in religious care. The medieval nunneries often provided care that families were unable or unwilling to provide.

Care was conceived of in terms of spiritual or moral care. People who came to **ministries** could expect little in terms of cure but a lot of care related to moral well being and religion, and a degree of care related to comfort.

Ministries
Religious orders made up of and controlled by nuns or monks

The religious structure of mother superior and sisters has been applied to secular nursing organisations in matrons (the roots of this word are to be found in the French word for mother) and sisters. Florence Nightingale based a lot of her structure for nursing on that of the religious orders.

ACTIVITY 15	ALLOW 10 MINUTES

1 Consider three or four main responsibilities ascribed to the caring function.

2 Consider a profile of behaviours expected of someone in the caring role.

THE ROOTS OF CARE

Responsibilities	Behaviours

Commentary

Your list might look something like the following:

Responsibilities	Behaviours
To the patient	Uncomplaining
To look after family members	To do whatever is required
To be there	To fulfil many roles
Not to complain	Sacrifice

The important issue to grasp here is that particular images or metaphors are associated with caring. If you relate the images of religious care to informal care you can begin to build up a picture of a carer as someone who:

- does not complain

- accepts their lot

- carries out their role due to some sense of duty

- expects no rewards

But these expectations in today's world can lead to psychological difficulties and burdens for carers.

Many professional and informal carers do not fit this stereotype of a nun. However, the formal carers may do so because of public expectations and professional boundaries. Formal carers act within well-defined boundaries. At the end of the shift they can go home and leave the roles and frustrations of the day behind them. Informal carers have no such boundaries and carry out roles associated with a number of professional groups.

The following quote from a carer illustrates this. She is talking about herself and her husband as carers for their disabled child.

> 'It's a life time's employment with no holiday pay or overtime for unsocial hours! I wonder if I will ever do anything myself again. Twenty-four hours is not enough in the day. We both need to be occupational therapists, speech therapists, psychotherapists; we have to get stroppy with the authorities to get what we want.'
> (SCOPE, 1995)

4: Care in the community

The attempt to relocate care in the community has consequences for those delivering the services, whether they be professional or informal carers. We will look at the impact of such changes on individuals in Session Five. For the moment, we will explore the structure within which care is delivered.

In 1981, Margaret Thatcher, then Prime Minister and architect of these changes, said:

> 'the statutory services are the supportive ones, underpinning
> where necessary, filling the gaps and helping the helpers'.
> (Jones, 1994)

This statement has an important ideological meaning. The state as the statutory sector is no longer viewed as the main source of care services. Such care is to be provided by the family or community and supported by the statutory services. There is no discussion as to what carers, or those receiving the care, feel or think about such changes, or how these will impact on their lives.

Many have commented that such changes are led purely by economic factors. While this may be so, it is also important to realise there is an ideology underpinning these changes.

This session has suggested that many of the ideas of a caring community of the past are based on a rose-tinted image of the past rather than on reality. These images or metaphors are powerful influences on policy development and the way in which care is delivered. The notion of consumerism as an ideology has permeated the provision of caring services and the use of words such as the following have become commonplace:

- providers of health and social care

- purchasers of care

- care package

- consumers

- empowerment.

With the provision of care and support to informal carers it is important to untangle who is being served. Many discourses on supporting carers neglect to mention the person being cared for (Titmuss, 1968). The focus is not on providing services directly to the person requiring care but on supporting the informal carer in what is seen as their role and their duty. This has led to what is now known as the mixed economy of care.

5: The mixed economy of care

The mixed economy of care was first suggested in the Griffiths Report (1988). It has been translated into practice by the Conservative government's encouragement of the private sector to provide care and support services. In 1993 Dr Brian Mawhinney, then Minister for Health, stated that:

'The .... requirements that local authorities spend at least 85% of the transfer element of the Special Transitional Grant in the independent sector is an important measure..... to ensure the development of a truly mixed economy'. (Leat, 1993)

The important point here is that the development of the independent sector is not being left to chance. A deliberate attempt is being made to manage the market, with an emphasis on shifting resources to the independent sector.

The idea that the independent sector can provide services more efficiently and cheaply than the statutory sector is a common one. The idea that the independent sector is more innovative than the statutory sector is also prevalent (Twigg, 1992).

The independent sector consists of voluntary groups, charities, non-profit making organisations and profit making organisations. Statements by the Conservative government make it clear, however, that the independent sector they envisage is the private, or profit making, sector.

The effect of introducing a market into the provision of care services may have an impact on all these organisations, both voluntary and private. The voluntary sector is being encouraged to become entrepreneurial and commercially-based in its outlook. The assumption is that the independent, for-profit sector can and will provide services in all areas of need. However, the reality of for-profit organisations in the independent sector is that they will only provide care where profit is possible.

ACTIVITY 16   ALLOW 50 MINUTES

Think of the various organisations which provide services to people who are HIV positive and people with AIDS. Make a list of those at national level and then list the local groups which provide a service. If you're not familiar with the services look them up in a directory or ask for help. Divide all the services into the following categories:

- statutory services

- voluntary services

- independent, for-profit groups or companies.

When you have done this compile similar lists of services for older people in your area.

Local and national services for people with AIDS/HIV

Local and national services for older people

Commentary

Your list of national organisations which provide services to people who are HIV positive or who have AIDS may have included organisations such as the health education authority, the Terence Higgins Trust, the National Aids Trust and the Department of Health. The local list may have included local statutory services such as a specialist HIV team, the local health promotion unit, the gastro-urinary medicine service at a local hospital and a whole range of voluntary agencies.

The national bodies providing care for the elderly will include Age Concern. Locally they will include local trusts, the local authority, private nursing homes and various local charity schemes funded from a number of different sources.

The service provision overall spans a wide range of organisations, from statutory to voluntary sector to private provision. The difference between the two areas (care for the elderly and HIV/AIDS care) is that there is little or no private sector provision for people with HIV/AIDS. The reasons for this are many, but for the moment we will focus on two :

- the nature of the illness
- the profit motive.

The nature of the disease is perceived as terminal although the span from infection to development of AIDS can be up to 15 years. There is little profit to be made from providing care to people with HIV and this, combined with the stigma of AIDS, makes it unattractive to private or for-profit agencies. This explains why the provision of care in the area of HIV has occurred through the development of charitable or voluntary agencies rather than through the independent, for-profit sector.

Encouraging a mixed economy of care doesn't mean that the market can be left to regulate itself. Otherwise the 'Cinderella services', such as those for people with HIV/AIDS, would not get attention or services. The independent sector would only provide services from which it can make a profit. The mixed economy of care is therefore not of universal application. In addition, there are indications that many would not want health and welfare services provided solely on the basis of profit.

Because of the introduction of market economies into health and welfare services, some of the distinctions between charitable/voluntary groups and the private, for-profit organisations are blurring. Organisations now have to enter into competition for services, regardless of whether they are profit or non-profit making organisations. For many voluntary organisations, the winning of service contracts is important as they use the income to subsidise other services.

The effects of the mixed economy of care

The mixed economy of care has important implications for the psychological profile of those delivering and receiving the services.

ACTIVITY 17   ALLOW **25** MINUTES

A local Age Concern group has been successful in its bid for a £0.5 million contract to provide a 'meals on wheels' service. This means that many of its voluntary workers will now be employed on a part-time basis and paid for the work they originally did free as volunteers.

Consider how the change will affect the different groups involved and write brief notes under each of the headings below:

1   Changes in the relationship between the agency and volunteers.

2   Changes in the relationship between volunteers and those receiving care.

3   Changes in the relationship between the agency and the statutory services, such as local trusts, GPs and gerontology services in the local hospital.

Commentary

The volunteers are now employees of the agency. This implies a change in their relationship with the Age Concern group. They may see their pay as a positive change in that it is a formal recognition of the work the volunteers/employees do. But it may mean the volunteers/employees are less able to criticise the workings of the agency. By becoming employees and receiving recognition for their roles, the former volunteers are part of the formal system of care. They become formal carers and their role changes.

The change in role may initially be hard but is likely to boost the self-confidence and image of the agency and the workers. It may also bring about dissension within the organisation. Some of its members and volunteers may object to the change in role, viewing it as a betrayal of what they believe in.

It may also change the way the people receiving care view their relationship with the former volunteers. For example, they may treat the former volunteers less as confidants and instead see them as people doing a job of work. The users or recipients of the service may view the agency itself in a different light. They may see it less as a source through which to channel their views or as an organisation which represents them and more as just another provider of services.

The psychology and profile of the agency may also be affected. Where previously it represented and spoke on behalf of those to whom it provided services, now it is part of the formal bureaucratic structure, and will need to fulfil the terms of its contract. The roles of advocate and officially appointed service provider do not fit easily together. You cannot bite the hand that feeds you.

The relationship between the agency and other providers of services will also be affected. If people believe that care is best delivered by the private, for-profit sector, other workers in both the voluntary and statutory sectors may feel that they are not recognised or rewarded for the work they do. This may lead to low self-esteem. Some studies have reflected this loss of morale in workers in the National Health Service.

We can see, then, that changes in role will have intrinsic effects on the psychological profiles of individuals and the agency. We will explore this further in Session Six when we look at the role of voluntary groups.

Summary

1 In looking at the development of, and changing patterns in, care services we have explored the role of community services and the family in the provision of care. Additionally, we considered some of the images and historical trends in care.

2 Historically, the notions of care are rooted in carers being self-sacrificing and uncomplaining. Some of the 'beliefs' concerning the family as the caring unit were challenged.

3 Images and myths surrounding modern ideas of care affect the psychological profiles and behaviours of carers as they attempt to live up to expectations.

4 The current emphasis on the mixed economy of care as a mode of delivery was explored.

Before you move on to Session Three, check that you have achieved the objectives given at the beginning of this session, and, if not, review the appropriate sections.

SESSION THREE

The psychology of care

Introduction

In the first two sessions we explored the evolution of care services and looked at the major influences on the role of the carer. This session builds on this by exploring in more detail how outside factors influence the psychology of individual carers, and how these factors interact.

This session presents a model of care from a psychological perspective. As with any model, it is a way of making sense of reality; it is not reality in itself. The model is made up of three perspectives:

- the caring role

- the psychology of the carer

- the responsibilities of caring.

We will examine each of these individually in this session and go on to explore how they interact and are interdependent in Session Seven.

Session objectives

When you have completed this session you should be able to:

- examine critically and give examples of factors that influence the psychology of the carer

- examine critically and give examples of factors that influence the psychology of the caring role

- examine critically and give examples of factors that influence the responsibilities of the carer

- discuss and give examples of the interactions between these three elements.

1: The caring role

While many factors influence the caring role, we are going to focus on those which impact on the psychology of the carer.

The three perspectives we are going to look at can be shown as circles with overlaps as in the Venn diagram shown in *Figure 3*.

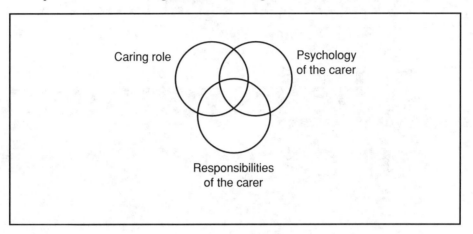

Figure 3: Responsibilities of the carer

We will look at each of these perspectives in turn and use a fishbone diagram to show the factors that make up each one.

Caring is a role not an occupation. It alters the way we view ourselves and the way others view us. We have already talked about how certain factors make it more likely that someone will be a carer. These factors include:

- gender – more likely if female

- spouse

- class

- relationship (usually family)

- financial resources.

Bear in mind that if you are female and related to the person requiring care, you are more likely to be a carer than if you are male and related to the person.

Such factors combine to influence the nature of the caring role. We can use a fishbone structure as a model to represent the role (see *Figure 4*). The 'bones' contribute to the backbone or central core of what it means to be a carer.

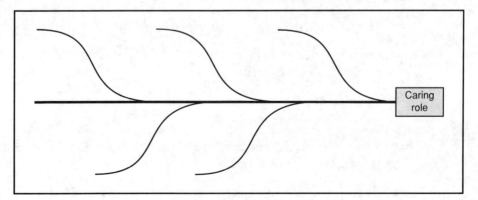

Figure 4: Model of the caring role

ACTIVITY 18   ALLOW **10** MINUTES

Using the fishbone structure below (*Figure 5*) fill in examples of what might constitute the 'feeder tributaries' or 'bones'. Add more tributaries or bones to the diagram if you want to include more examples.

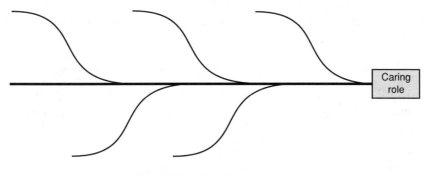

Figure 5: Model of the caring role

Commentary

Your examples might include the following:

relationship to person being cared for

gender

age

capability

financial means and resources.

See *Figure 6*. The model is flexible in that it can accommodate the generic role of caring and can also be applied to individual caring situations. There is no one right answer as each individual situation will demand that different factors be placed on the tributaries.

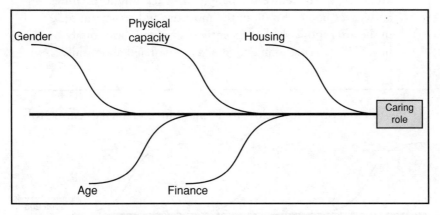

Figure 6: Feeder tributaries of the caring role

ACTIVITY 19   ALLOW **25** MINUTES

Read the following two case studies and fill in the fishbone structure at the end of each one.

CASE STUDY 2

James and **Jenny** have been married for 40 years. They are now both in their late 70s. For the last five years James has looked after Jenny as she displayed the early signs of dementia. James has arthritis which limits the physical care he can give. He receives support from the district nurse and the home help.

Now fill in the fishbone structure identifying the aspects which contribute to and limit James's role. When you have done this move on to Case Study 3.

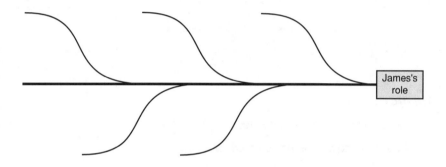

Figure 7: James's caring role

CASE STUDY 3

Margaret is a 16-year-old girl with Down syndrome. She cares for herself and, like most teenagers, requires occasional reminding to look after herself. She has recently started attending a day centre for people with learning difficulties and leaves home at 8.00 in the morning and returns at 5.30 in the afternoon. She has recently started talking a lot about boys. Her parents John and Sheila are worried about this.

Use the fishbone structure below to define John and Sheila's caring role.

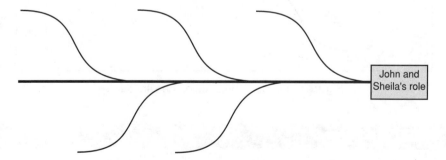

Figure 8: John and Sheila's caring role

Commentary

These two case studies show the differing nature of caring roles. The roles are dependent not just on the needs of the individual but also on the abilities of the carer. Caring roles are not defined in absolute terms but depend on a whole host of factors. *Figures 9* and *10* show suggested fishbone diagrams for both case studies.

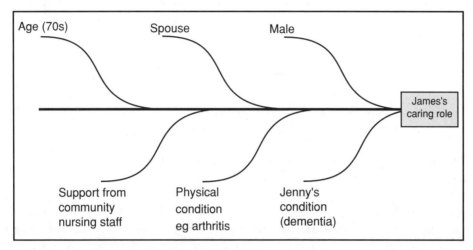

Figure 9: James's caring role

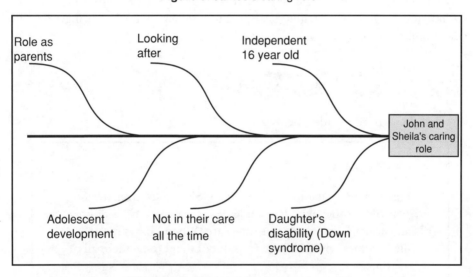

Figure 10: John and Sheila's caring role

You can see that the general factors which influence the caring role become specific when applied to individual cases. So the relationship in James's situation is based on being married to Jenny, while John and Sheila's relationship is that of parents.

2: The psychology of the carer

The psychology of the carer is influenced by a number of issues, such as past relationship to the person being cared for, experience, expectations, feelings of power, self-image and gender.

Again these issues can be combined in a fishbone structure as shown in *Figure 11*.

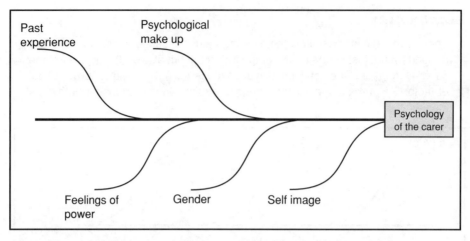

Figure 11: Diagrammatic representation of the psychology of the carer

It is important to point out that we are talking about psychology in relation to the caring role, not the general psychological profile of the individual. However, it is likely that an individual's general psychological make-up will affect their role as carer. At the same time, the caring role may affect their general psychological make up. For example, someone with a generally positive outlook on life may change through their experience of being a carer. The demands and frustrations may make them irritable and change their outlook to one of pessimism. The way an individual's general psychological profile interacts with the caring role will depend on the situation.

ACTIVITY 20

ALLOW 25 MINUTES

Read the two case studies below.

CASE STUDY 4

Jane is a 38-year-old single woman. She looks after her 80-year-old mother who has senile dementia and who is doubly incontinent. She needs full-time care. When Jane is not there she becomes upset, so Jane feels duty-bound to be there all of the time.

CASE STUDY 5

Susan is a 38-year-old woman whose 15-year-old son John is wheelchair bound. He lives at home and attends a day school. He leaves early in the morning and returns around 4.00pm. Two out of every four weekends are spent on activities organised by the school such as adventure weekends. Sometimes Susan goes with John on these weekends, but due to her wide circle of friends and interests she is not always free to go. John cares for himself and needs only occasional help with bathing and transport.

How much does the caring role impact on the lives and identities of the carers in these case studies?

Commentary

You might agree that Jane's role as a carer is all-consuming and occupies all her time, while for Susan it is certainly part of her life (an important one) but it does not dominate or consume it. These two cases are represented diagrammatically in *Figures 12a and 12b*. In both diagrams the psychological profile is directly related to the amount of the carer's life which is taken up by the caring role.

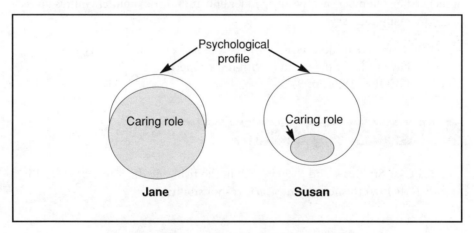

Figures 12 a and b: Psychological profile

In Jane's case the caring role goes a long way to defining or making up her psychological profile. This is shown in *Figure 12a* as the caring role takes up a large part of the circle representing her psychological profile. In contrast, Susan's caring role (in *Figure 12b*) plays a smaller part in contributing to and influencing her psychological profile.

The flow of influences works both ways. Both Susan's and Jane's psychological make-up will feed into their psychological roles as carers.

Different situations make different contributions to the caring role. Caring for disabled children is different from caring for children who are expected to get better or at least rehabilitated for the following reasons:

- it is a long-term responsibility

- the long-term outlook for disabled children differs from that for non-disabled children

- discrimination against disabled people is apparent.

The long-term outlook for disabled children is bleak, not necessarily because of the child's disability, but because of the limited opportunities available to disabled people to lead independent lives.

It is important to remember that there are both positive and negative aspects to caring and that these will impact on the psychological profile. The following two quotes illustrate this:

> 'How do I feel as a carer? As if I've been thrown into prison by society.'

> 'My life is enriched in many unexpected and wonderful ways because of our life together'.

The psychology of the carer will be influenced by a whole range of factors. It is the interaction of those factors with the psychology of the carer that is the important issue. It is a two-way process: the individual is not a blank sheet waiting to be 'written on' by those factors.

3: The responsibility of caring

The factors that contribute to the responsibilities of carers are not just the physical aspects of caring, but also the emotional, power and support issues. These are influenced in a number of ways, by gender and guilt, for example. Guilt is an issue raised by many carers:

> 'I do have to do physio with her and feel extremely guilty if I haven't had time to do it with her properly'.
> (SCOPE, 1995, p. 9)

ACTIVITY 21   ALLOW **15** MINUTES

Read Case Studies 4 and 5 again. Fill in the fishbone diagrams (*Figures 13 and 14* below) to show each carer's responsibilities.

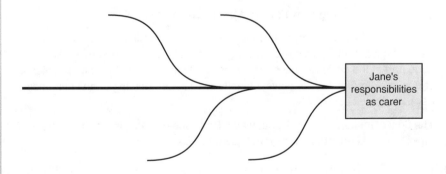

Jane's responsibilities as carer

Figure 13 : Jane's responsibilities as carer

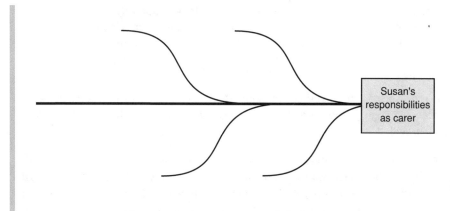

Figure 14 : Susan's responsibilities as carer

Commentary

You have probably recognised that Jane's responsibilities are more demanding and difficult than Susan's. Jane also apparently has less control over the situation.

Figures 15 and 16 are suggested fishbone diagrams showing Jane's and Susan's responsibilities as caring roles.

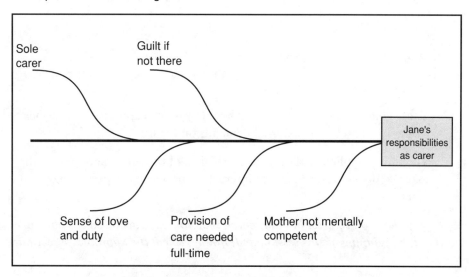

Figure 15 : Jane's responsibilities as carer

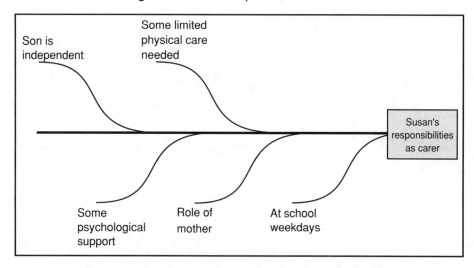

Figure 16 : Susan's responsibilities as carer

Susan's responsibilities are less onerous than Jane's. John (Susan's son) has mobility and access problems, but aside from these her responsibilities are the same as those of any mother with a teenage son. Jane, on the other hand, is bound by her responsibilities. Of course, at some level she is choosing to be bound by them.

The provision of extra resources for support and sitting services may ease Jane's burden, although it is not clear whether she would make use of them even if these were provided.

People come to caring relationships with attitudes and psychological profiles which have already been shaped. The activity of caring will further interact with these attitudes, values and psychological traits. They are not necessarily fixed, but do have an influence on future attitudes and behaviour.

The caring relationship should ultimately be a healthy one. A healthy caring relationship is one in which the three components of our model of the psychology of care come together and interrelate with each other. In Session Seven we will explore interaction between the various elements of the model in depth.

Summary

1 We have explored the psychology of care focusing on three perspectives or components:

   a) caring role

   b) psychology of the carer

   c) responsibilities of the carer.

   These components are influenced by the way the carer views his or her caring role and by the external demands on the carer.

2 The forces implicit within the caring role and those emanating from the external demands on the carer interact to influence the psychology of the carer.

Before you move on to Session Four, check that you have achieved the objectives given at the beginning of this session and, if not, review the appropriate sections.

The psychology of roles

Introduction

In previous sessions we have looked at:

- what care is

- the historical implications of the development of care

- a psychological model of care.

In this session we explore the role, behaviour and mindset of carers. A lot of the work in this session draws on the ideas of Carl Rogers, an American psychologist, and the theories of transactional analysis. The main idea used is that of scripts and script development. You will find a list of recommended reading in the section on further reading.

Session objectives

When you have completed this session you should be able to:

- examine critically and give examples of role development and role casting

- give examples of the usefulness of roles in the caring relationship

- examine critically the positive and negative 'strokes' and feedback that carers receive

- give examples of the negative aspects of role casting or occupation in formal and informal care settings

- discuss critically the inter relationships between various roles in the caring situation

- critically examine the role relationships between formal and informal carers

- reflect on the problems in role relationships between formal and informal carers and the potential for conflict which can arise in relation to who the client is within these role relationships.

1: Introduction to roles

In Session Three we showed that caring is not simply about giving care but that it is also about the roles, responsibilities and duties that go with it. The role of carer, whether formal or informal, has key components. The rewards, recognitions, frustrations and pain that different roles provide differ in their nature, quality and quantity but not in principle.

We are not suggesting that there is a psychological profile which fits all carers and that this is a world of stereotypes. Rather, the suggestion is that the role of carer has certain demands, obligations and rewards attached to it. The extent to which any individual carer occupies a role depends on their individual psychological profile and the constraints and opportunities they face.

Think back to the case studies in Session Three. The types of pressures and demands faced by the carers are similar. What differs is each individual's response to these demands and pressures. These responses are influenced by an individual's psychological profile and also by the resources available to them.

We have said that roles are not just an occupation. The SCOPE (1995) report on carers suggests that:

'caring is a role, not just an occupation, because it alters the way in which people are viewed by others and by themselves'.

Adopting a caring role can have repercussions beyond the responsibilities and obligations to perform physical tasks. For example:

'It confers membership to a marginalised group'.
(SCOPE, 1995)

Roles can be occupied on a permanent or temporary basis. Some individuals have many roles, others have only one or two.

Another way of thinking of roles is by using the idea of 'masks'. The eminent American psychologist Carl Rogers talked about individuals wearing masks. Masks are what we wear to hide our real selves. We may wear different masks in different areas of our lives. It is possible, for example, for a man to be very assertive and competent at work while being passive and unassertive at home.

ACTIVITY 22   ALLOW **20** MINUTES

CASE STUDY 6

Jane is an extremely busy mother. She lives with her husband John and three children (ages 12, 8 and 7). She works in a

> local building society and manages five staff.
>
> Two evenings a week she goes to the local further education college to study for her banking exams. She still plays in her local basketball team: she has been a member since she left secondary school. They compete in a local league about once a month.

Can you identify at least three of Jane's roles or masks, as Rogers calls them? Write down your ideas.

Commentary

Jane's roles include :

- partner to John
- mother to children
- worker
- student
- competitor.

You may have identified Jane's caring role in her family. Although in this case it is not dominant, it is certainly an important part of her life. You can see that Jane leads a life with lots of roles in it. The roles are not all separate: there are relationships and links between the various elements. Jane's psychological profile contributes to the roles and the roles contribute to her psychological profile. Some would argue that her roles and activities are chosen (maybe unconsciously) to suit her psychological profile. So she may have chosen to be a mother to meet her psychological needs about caring. She may play basketball to meet a competition need or just because it's fun.

Not everyone chooses what they wish to do. Some people take on roles without having a choice. Roles occupied by choice result in a more positive psychological profile than those we are forced to occupy.

The following quote shows the range of roles a carer may have to occupy:

> 'I'm mum, dad, doctor, nurse..... playmate.... (and) told by my mates that I'm a state scrounger'.
> (SCOPE, 1995)

These roles may involve considerable effort and take up time. But caring and the caring role, while demanding, also have rewards. This is what we will now explore.

Positive and negative aspects of caring roles

> **CASE STUDY 7**
>
> **Alice** has recently returned home to the small village in which she was brought up to look after her mother. Her father, who recently died, was the main carer for her mother who is 74, immobile but mentally alert. Alice has given up her job as a personal assistant to the managing director of a small firm. The director was sorry to see her go and promised to keep her job open for nine months in case she returned. Her brother who is married visits once a month with his family and contributes some financial help.

Consider the issues about the role Alice occupies and the options she faces. Also think about the positive and negative aspects of her caring role. Note down your ideas.

Commentary

This case study highlights the pressures women face in fulfilling caring roles. Alice may have felt a sense of duty to provide care. This is more prevalent among daughters than sons and is something that is socially dictated. It is not necessarily a psychological trait, but the behaviour of a carer is influenced by this social expectation. Men are expected to 'care about' rather than 'care for' members of their families.

Many aspects of the caring role are intimate in nature, requiring touch, invasion of boundaries and contact with human excreta. These are associated with the domestic roles traditionally occupied by women. One of the consequences of this is that a man undertaking such tasks is more likely to be viewed as a carer and receive support from various agencies. This is because his role is regarded as unusual.

Women undertaking such roles are expected to absorb them into their domestic roles. Twigg and Atkin (1993) found that a home care organiser would automatically establish home help support to a working man, but would have to think about it for a working woman. The consequences of such actions are that working women are more likely to have to give up their jobs to care for relatives or spouses.

Alice had options, but not necessarily easy ones. She could have considered getting help for her mother from the local authority or putting her in a home. Many people balk at such measures saying things like 'I can't imagine a stranger looking after her'.

If Alice is a reluctant carer she may feel pressured into looking after her mother and angry at giving up her life. She may have exchanged many roles or masks for the dominant one of a carer. This may have an effect on her psychological health and indeed on the caring relationship with her mother. Her feelings of anger and resentment may manifest themselves in her behaviour towards her mother.

Respite holiday cover is sometimes provided to alleviate such feelings, to enable informal carers to continue in their roles. A respite holiday enables the cared for person to be cared for by others so that the main carer can have a rest .

Many carers feel positive about their lives and their decision to be a carer. The positive aspect of Alice's role may be that she is performing a function for someone she loves. The rewards may lie in doing a useful task, keeping her mother out of institutional care and helping her to stay in her own home.

The positive feedback people get from performing a role is sometimes called 'positive strokes'. However, carers can be positive about their role, and still feel tired, bored and isolated. The following responses by carers were identified in a recent SCOPE report (1995):

Tired	82%
Frustrated	77%
Worried	71%
Emotionally stressed	68%
Angry	60%
Isolated	40%
Unwell	40%
Lonely	34%
Guilty	27%
Despair	25%

These are in contrast to the positive feelings identified, which were:

Happy	42%
Proud	41%
Complete	31%
Confident	27%
In control	27%

These responses all came from the same sample. You will notice there are more negative than positive responses. Positive and negative elements can co-exist; so you might be proud of your role but also tired and worried. The positive and negative feelings can also exist in combination; so you may feel proud but tired because of all the demands of the task and angry because of the lack of recognition of your role.

ACTIVITY 24   ALLOW 20 MINUTES

Read over Alice's story in Activity 23. Some additional information is that the district nurse visits twice a week and that, on two mornings, a home help comes to help with basic chores.

Describe the roles Alice, the district nurse and the home help play. Then make a list of the positive and negative aspects of their respective roles.

	Alice as informal carer	district nurse	home help
Role			
Positive aspects			
Negative aspects			

Commentary

The roles and their positive and negative aspects are suggested in *Table 2* below:

	Alice as informal carer	district nurse	home help
Role	Informal carer, not trained, non-professional, full-time.	Formal carer, trained. Professional support and care to Alice and her mother.	Formal carer, skilled, support to Alice and her mother.

	Alice as informal carer	district nurse	home help
Positive aspects	Encouragement from professionals. Family recognition of her role.	Useful job helping others. Role as professional.	Useful job helping others. Role as professional.
Negative aspects	No pay. Lack of public recognition. Too much work.	Ungrateful clients.	Ungrateful clients.

Table 2: Positive and negative aspects of caring roles

The difference between the roles of these people is that Alice's role has the potential to be all-consuming, taking up her time, apart from short breaks given by the formal carers, and having a major effect on the way she perceives herself. The district nurse and the home help occupy a number of roles apart from their professional one. At the end of the day's work they go home and occupy another role.

The advantage of having different roles is that they offer a break or respite in psychological terms. Sometimes this may just be a displacement activity. Having a respite from a caring role doesn't make the problem go away. It allows the mind a break or a rest from the trials it faces.

Some of the strategies the mind uses to deal with stressful situations are:

- denial
- repression
- sublimination
- projection
- transference
- depression
- palliative techniques.

The strategies listed, apart from the palliative techniques, are what Freud called ego defence mechanisms. They may be conscious or unconscious. They are intra-psychic, or internal, in their focus and while they protect the individual from a psychological viewpoint, they do little to change the situation carers are facing. Here are some examples of ego defence mechanisms that people use:

- **denial** – 'there is no problem, I can cope'
- **repression** –'I don't have a problem'
- **projection** – 'the government/the social workers are to blame'.

For further explanation consult one of the psychological textbooks listed in the further reading section.

Palliative techniques aim to deal with the symptoms of stress. They usually manifest themselves in terms of behaviours to mask the symptoms. The more common ones are smoking, drinking, overeating and hyperactivity. These activities deal with the physiological effects of stress or distress (Bunting, 1989; Robinson, 1988).

There are two ways of dealing with a problem. The first is by changing your view or psychological interpretation of the problem. This requires you to play down the psychological cost to yourself so you can adapt by thinking this is your lot as a carer. This allows you to accept the burden of caring. This is not to suggest that you are happy with it. Stress or, more accurately, distress occurs when the individual cannot reconcile the various aspects of a situation because an imbalance occurs. Very often this imbalance in the psychological health of an individual carer manifests itself in some physical way, so carers under stress have high rates of physical illness.

The presence of abuse is sometimes seen as an indication of stress. Remember here we are not talking about sexual abuse or physical abuse of minors, but the sort of abuse which might result when a carer out of frustration abuses some one they love and care for (Douglas et al., 1980, Lau and Kosberg, 1978).

Two other avenues for this imbalance to express itself are in either physical or psychological illness. These can be seen as the individual's way of adapting to the stress or distress.

The second, more successful way of dealing with the situation is by direct action. This is not necessarily the same as solving the problem but it does imply action by the individual to do something about the situation. It requires an individual to marshal their resources and to act on them. This boosts an individual's self-esteem and sense of power, thus improving the sense of psychological health.

It is important to note that this can sometimes backfire. If an individual engages in direct action and is determined to succeed, then failure can damage the individual's psychological health. As in assertiveness work, the issue is to make people feel better about themselves. The end outcome is not to 'win' or to get your way but to act in situations where you would not formerly have acted and to feel better about having been assertive. We will look at this issue in more depth in Session Seven.

2: Who is the client? – role relationships

The Community Care Monitoring Report for 1994 (DOH, 1995) noted the conflict between carers and users:

> 'others commented on the potential for conflict between the needs of users and carers; and the confusion created for staff who were attempting to deal with carers as partners in care but also as users of services'.
> (DOH, 1995, p. 16)

Those who are informal carers may therefore occupy two roles; partners in care and clients of formal carers. In the Case Study in Activities 23 and 24, Alice is involved with the district nurse as a partner in providing care services. She may also at some point receive services from the district nurse herself, perhaps through counselling or support, thus becoming a client of the formal carer (district nurse).

This can lead to conflict, both in roles and in communication. The working relationship between formal and informal carers ranges along a continuum from partners in care to a passive role for informal carers, as shown in *Figure 17*.

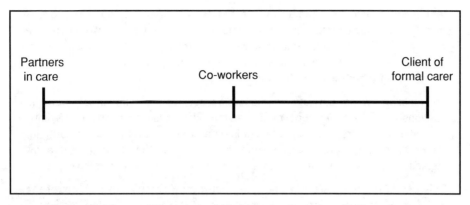

Figure 17: The working relationship between formal and informal carers

The roles people 'act out' depend on where they are on this continuum. The important point to bear in mind is that informal carers have two relationships with formal carers. The roles are not mutually exclusive and there is an overlap between the two. The problem for the formal carer is in separating out the roles. At one stage the formal and informal carers could be operating in a partnership arrangement in the delivery of care, while at another point the relationship could involve the formal carer offering care to the informal carer.

The roles and relationships of volunteers should also be considered. Volunteers, whether engaged in personal care or social support, will occupy different roles and wear different masks as appropriate (Wilmott and Thomas, 1994).

This raises the question of what sorts of care it is reasonable for different types of carers to deliver.

ACTIVITY 25 — ALLOW 15 MINUTES

Write down what you think to be reasonable tasks for a volunteer, for an informal carer and for a formal carer in the care of a five-year-old with cystic fibrosis.

volunteer

informal carer

formal carer

Commentary

The distinction between what care it is reasonable for these different carers to carry out depends either on their relationship or their training. Tasks requiring intimacy either require training or a close relationship with the carer. For the formal carer this constitutes a role. We allow professionals in their roles to look after us. The same professional may experience difficulty in providing care to a relative. For example, a district nurse who performs functions and procedures of an intimate nature with her patients may encounter difficulty in performing the same tasks for her own elderly mother.

The functions we perform and the roles we occupy overlap. With formal carers the relationship is of a professional nature, so the intimacy is similarly defined by this. The intimacy a nurse has with a client is different from the intimacy a daughter brings to the caring role with her mother or father. Professional roles allow distance to be kept between the carer and the person being cared for.

This overlap is not always a bad thing but it may complicate aspects of the caring role. Informal carers, occupying a number of roles in a caring encounter, may have to provide the gamut of activities from emotional support through advocacy to that of a physical carer. The situation may be less complicated for a volunteer, as in some ways they have more in common with the nurse than the informal carer.

The distinction between caring for people in need and caring about them has been made by a number of writers (Allan 1985; Higgins 1989). Caring about people can be viewed as love and caring for can be seen as labour or task orientated.

Most formal care can be conceptualised as 'caring for', incorporating an element of 'caring about' (see *Figure 18a* below). Informal care is defined by the concept of 'caring about', incorporating an element of 'caring for' or physical tasks (see *Figure 18b*). *Figure 18* shows that the main part of the role of the formal carer is the physical act of caring for someone. Within this may be an element of caring on a personal basis about the individual, as is presented by the inner circle. With informal care the opposite is true. The main part of the role is the caring about relationship and this has an impact on the caring for relationship: and as we have seen may complicate it.

It is important to note that the diagrams do not represent the amount of work involved in the caring for relationship. They represent conceptually the relationship between formal carers and informal carers and how these can be distinguished by means of the roles involved

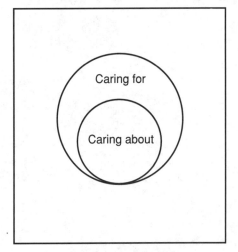

Figure 18a: Formal carers

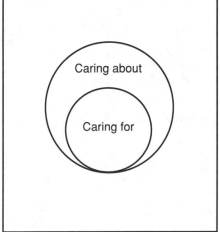

Figure 18b: Informal carers

3: Role casting

Identifying with a role is a way of dealing with stressful situations. Consider your own job and your dealings with the public. You can probably think of situations where you have been aware of your 'role' as nurse, district nurse, home help or social worker, rather than of your role as an individual. When in one role we react differently than we would in another. Some roles give us power and responsibility and others disempower us.

Ascribing roles is called 'role casting'. Sometimes the role and the behaviour associated with it are more dominant than the psychological profile of the individual. A model of psychology called transactional analysis likens this to being cast in a film or play.

Transactional analysis suggests that life is similar to a play in which we act out what the roles demand of us. Even when someone rebels against the role, they are still being influenced by it.

In transactional analysis this is called a script (Jongeward and James, 1994). When in role you follow a script. The script for carers is influenced by factors such as gender and relationship to the person being cared for.

ACTIVITY 26 — ALLOW 10 MINUTES

Imagine the role of a carer in a play or TV drama. Jot down a history of the role and the characterisation for the part. What are the major influences on the role of carer? How does the character react with other characters in the script?

Commentary

This activity should have helped you begin to get the idea of roles, scripts and masks. Spend a couple of moments reflecting on your own role as a carer and how it follows a script. Ask yourself: what are the major influences on your role as a carer? Also think about how others type-cast or stereotype you in your role.

Roles of defence

Roles have advantages as well as negative aspects. Carers can use roles or masks to protect themselves. By having a number of masks the individual has a number of aspects to his/her personality and doesn't have to be dependent on one. The role or mask allows individuals to adopt a certain aspect of behaviour and to take shelter behind it. This is a form of protection. It may be particularly important in caring roles which require a change in the relationship.

CASE STUDY 8

George has come to live with his daughter Susan. Until recently, he lived on his own. He lost his wife, Beth, five years ago. Since then he has looked after himself and has been fiercely independent. Recently the neighbours have noticed some changes in his behaviour. He has become unkempt and has started walking the streets at night. He has been diagnosed as suffering from pre-senile dementia.

Since he moved in with Susan she has experienced difficulty in her dealings with him. He sometimes soils himself and has to be reminded to go to the toilet and bathe himself. On a number of occasions she has had to bathe him herself. She has found this difficult.

Although she has always had a close relationship with her father it was never the kind where they would hug and cuddle. Now she finds it embarrassing to have to remind him about bathing and toileting. She is also embarrassed by having to wash him as she finds it 'awful' touching his genitals and even seeing him in the nude. She has noticed that her behaviour changes at these times. She becomes more brusque, using phrases like 'come along now' and acting in an offhand manner.

Analyse the above case study from the point of view of the changing roles of Susan and her father, identifying those roles which Susan is using as a form of defence.

Commentary

Susan has two roles in her relationship with her father; the role of daughter and the role of carer. She now seems to be using one aspect of her role as a carer in order to protect herself. A woman who has in the past been looked after by her father now finds the roles reversed. She is now caring for him but also providing care which is of an intimate nature. She appears to have adopted a role akin to a nurse in order to provide some psychological protection for herself. By adopting a nursing role she puts some distance between herself and her father. It is like wearing a mask to hide her real self.

Whether masks are worn intentionally or not is a moot point. Conscious use of masks or roles undoubtedly occurs. For example, on your way to a meeting you may find yourself acting out in your own mind what is going to occur and how you will tackle the issue.

By rehearsing the role you are more easily able to occupy it. Being assertive is something a lot of us find difficult, but by learning some skills we can occupy the role and wear the mask. The problem arises when we are unaware that we are in role or wearing a mask and it interferes with our lives in a negative way.

4: Shedding masks

The shedding of masks is not always easy for informal carers because the role is often so consuming. For formal carers changing out of a uniform is one way of shedding the caring role for another. The change of clothes symbolises this process.

However, there is evidence that informal carers have problems making the transition from care giving to bereavement when their loved one dies or is hospitalised (Bass and Bowman, 1990). This suggests that informal carers have difficulty shedding their role/mask. The difficulty may also be tied up with the removal of support on the death of the cared-for person. No services are available to help the carer through this stage or change in roles.

ACTIVITY 28   ALLOW 10 MINUTES

Thinking of role identification and behaviour, consider why it might be difficult for ex-carers to return to normal living and why it might be difficult for them to move into a bereavement role on the death of someone they care for. Write your suggestions down.

Commentary

Where ex-carers find it difficult to leave their role, it may be that their original role identification may have been so consuming that it accounts for their self-identity and their self-esteem. The behaviour of carers, whether they provide personal, domestic or auxiliary care, can further reinforce the role they occupy. There may be a certain congruence between role identification and behaviour. One reinforces the other.

Formal carers may be able to help informal carers make those transitions by providing support and counselling services.

Summary

1   You have looked at roles both in the way they provide some form of protection for carers and in the negative consequences they may have.

2   You have considered the extent to which roles occupy or make up an individual's psychology.

3   Shifting between roles or masks is a means of protecting our own identity and coping with those cared for. Without breaks caring roles can become all consuming and are the main form of self-identification.

4   Some find it difficult to mourn or become ex-carers because of the way they have occupied the caring role.

Before you move on to Session Five, check that you have achieved the objectives given at the beginning of this session and, if not, review the appropriate sections.

SESSION FIVE

Support for informal carers

Introduction

When the Griffiths Report (1988) put forward the notion of a 'mixed economy of care' it praised the role of informal carers but did not address the stress and psychological impact involved.

In order to understand the psychological impact of informal caring, we need to know:

- who the informal carers are

- what they do

- the positive and negative psychological effects of caring on them

- how networks and groups can provide psychological support.

We address these four areas in this session.

Session objectives

When you have completed this session you should be able to:

- describe the psychological impact of being an informal carer

- describe the kind of psychological support which informal carers may require

- give examples of approaches to informal carer support networks and groups and critically examine the impact these networks can have on the psychology of the carer.

1: Who are the informal carers and what do they do?

The last General House Survey (GHS) asked the respondents if they looked after or provided some regular service for someone who was 'sick, elderly or handicapped' (Green, 1988) either in their own home or elsewhere. More than 14 per cent of people in the survey over the age of sixteen indicated that they provided help in the way specified. This survey does not include data about how many children are carers to sick or disabled parents.

If this percentage is representative of the entire population of the UK, then it suggests that there are approximately six million carers.

The estimate of six million carers may be an exaggerated number in that not all carers identified in the GHS were the main carers. Some lived in the same household as the sick, elderly or disabled person whom they helped; others provided care for more than 20 hours per week, giving help and supervision. In addition other research shows that different people need different types of care and as a result there are different types of carers, doing different types of caring work and needing different types of support.

ACTIVITY 29 ALLOW 5 MINUTES

How would you define the term 'informal carer'? Write your definition here.

Commentary

The Carer's National Association defines a carer as anyone whose life is in some way restricted because of the need to take responsibility for the care of a person who is mentally ill, mentally handicapped, physically disabled or whose health is impaired by sickness or old age.

The key phrase is 'take responsibility' because it implies that the carer is the primary care giver and that the care being given may or may not be supported by outside public, private or voluntary agencies.

How did your definition compare with the one from the Carer's National Association?

ACTIVITY 30   ALLOW 20 MINUTES

Make a list of the types of 'caring tasks' which might be carried out by informal carers. Identify broad categories of caring tasks, such as help with physical activities, and take into account all types of illness, age groups and disabilities.

Commentary

You have probably listed a range of caring tasks. The GHS (Green, 1988) identified eight caring tasks:

1 Help with physical activities (e.g. walking, getting in or out of bed)

2 Help with personal care (e.g. dressing, bathing, toiletting)

3 Help with financial affairs and paperwork

4 Other practical help (e.g. working, shopping, household chores, repairs)

5 Keeping the person company

6 Taking the person out

7 Help related to medication or changing dressings

8 Keeping an eye on the person/seeing that the person is all right.

Parker and Lawton (1990) used these eight caring tasks to identify six quite specific care patterns.

a Personal and physical help (with or without other kinds of help)

b Personal but not physical help (with or without other kinds of help)

c Physical but not personal help (with or without other kinds of help)

d Practical help with at least one other form of help except personal or physical

e Practical help only

f Any other combinations of help.

This typology is helpful for two reasons. First, it helps us to differentiate between different types of help and different types of carers. The six patterns of care also identify six different types of carer. Second, the six types of care enable us to begin to look at the factors which are associated with having heavy involvement in care. Look back at the 'categories of care' in section 6 of Session One. How does the typology identified by Parker and Lawton (1990) compare with the categories in section 6?

ACTIVITY 31   ALLOW 20 MINUTES

If you were to identify what constitutes 'heavy involvement' in care by an informal carer, what factors or criteria might you use to differentiate between heavy involvement in care and superficial or light involvement in care? Write down your criteria.

Commentary

You may have come up with a number of factors or criteria for deciding what counts as being 'heavily involved' in caring for another person. Parker (1992) found that the following five factors were associated with identifying heavy involvement in care by informal carers:

- the hours for which carers provide assistance

- whether or not anyone else helps

- whether or not the carer lives in the same household as the person requiring care

- the number of different activities involved

- whether or not the person needing help has a mental impairment.

In addition, and perhaps more importantly, all of the above five factors are closely associated with personal and/or physical help. How does Parker's list of five factors compare with your list in Activity 31?

In summary, heavy involvement seems to rest primarily with those who give the major input into physical and/or personal care for another. Just how heavy that involvement is, is related to the other five factors.

Having looked at the criteria, it will be helpful to explore who the carers are who are 'heavily involved'.

Parker (1992) made four useful observations:

- except for those who care for people over the age of 85, carers tend to be more heavily involved with helping younger people than with elderly people

- the age of the informal carer is not a good predictor of heavy involvement, although carers over the age of 55 are somewhat more heavily involved in personal and/or physical care

- those who are informal carers for children (regardless of age) and spouses living in the same household are the most likely to be heavily involved in personal and/or physical care

- men are less likely than women to become informal carers although when they do, their experience of caring and the impact it has on their lives is not so very different to the experience of women. Approximately the same proportion of male carers are heavily involved in physical and/or personal care as female carers.

2: The positive and negative psychological effects of caring on informal carers

In this section we look at the positive and negative psychological effects of caring on informal carers, and then at the effects on children who are carers.

The positive psychological effects of caring

ACTIVITY 32   **ALLOW 20 MINUTES**

Think about what you have learned in the previous section 'who are the informal carers?'. Draw on your own experience to make a list of what you think the positive and negative psychological effects of informal caring might be.

Negative	Positive

Commentary

So much of the literature identifies negative psychological effects of caring that any positive effects often go ignored. Grant and Nolan (1993) found in their research that, for many, being a carer was often very satisfying and rewarding.

The evidence they present shows that caring can be a source of personal satisfaction for many informal carers and that this satisfaction leads to an increased self-esteem on the part of the carer which can co-exist and even balance out any high levels of stress. Their analysis seems to indicate, however, that the psychological rewards and satisfactions which exist in the informal caring role are the result of factors within the social context of care, rather than of the personal or dependency characteristics of the person being cared for.

This could indicate that the rewards and satisfactions felt by informal carers (who are largely women) might be as a result of the socialisation of women in society into caring roles and the fact that they are not expected to have negative feelings about those they care for (Dalley,1988).

Ungerson (1987) found that motivation in the informal caring role was very mixed and that some women find that caring gives them a source of female identity and joy. The male informal carers in the study had different motivations. Male carers conceptualise their carer role as a form of work and use the same occupational language to describe their role as that used in the labour market. Male carers also referred to their motivation for their caring role as love, as opposed to the female carers who described their motivation as duty.

Ungerson's study also showed that male carers felt that they needed to be in control or in a position of power over the person being cared for, while women who were carers were more likely to feel disempowered, powerless or controlled by the person for whom they were caring. Some male carers described their role positively as giving them a reason for living (Ungerson, 1987).

Some of the negative words which you might have included in your list are: stress, emotional strain/exhaustion, depression, powerlessness, loneliness/isolation. You may have included others as well.

The negative psychological effects of caring

There have been many studies to show that informal carers experience increased levels of stress or emotional strain as a result of their responsibilities as carers (for example, Clarkson et al., 1986; Quine and Pahl, 1989; Braithwaite, 1990). You may wish to read these studies to learn more about the research.

Parker (1992) suggests that the high levels of stress experienced by carers could mean that carers might be less able to continue caring over time.

Parker also reminds us that stress (and response to stress) is subjective and that people in the same situation may experience different degrees of stress. Stress can also be influenced by social or cultural expectations. Ungerson's study (1987) described the emotional exhaustion which the respondents experienced and their feelings of being 'trapped' by the duty they felt to the person for whom they cared. Many of Ungerson's subjects felt exploited and dehumanised, forced by social pressures into a role they did not want. Such feelings can lead to anger and resentment, and ultimately to stress.

The need to recognise stress and to provide assistance to carers to help them manage is important both to the carer and the person receiving care, since it is the severity of the stress experienced by the informal carer which determines whether the dependant remains at home or is institutionalised.

Twigg (1989) identified that caring imposes burdens and costs upon the informal carer. Hooyman et al. (1985) and Wright (1986) found that the role of informal caring can be highly disruptive to the carer's social and personal life. A whole range of research studies (for example, Brody, 1985; Gwyther and George, 1986; Bell et al., 1987; Thompson, 1987) has produced overwhelming evidence that the most prevalent and common consequence of caring is a deterioration in the emotional health of the carer. What is not quite so clear is which aspects of the carer role are most stressful and how this stress can be alleviated.

ACTIVITY 33   ALLOW 40 MINUTES

Read the article by Nolan, Grant and Ellis, *Resource 1* in the *Resources Section* at the back of the workbook.

What are the key factors leading to 'carer malaise' identified in this research? Write down your answers.

Commentary

Nolan, Grant and Ellis (1990) found that the following factors are important to the amount of stress experienced by a carer:

- the carer's perception of their caring role

- the extent to which they feel out of control of their situation

- the amount of guilt they experience

- the nature of their relationship with their dependant

- absence of family support.

How does this list compare with your answers? If you experienced difficulties, return to the article, focusing primarily on the discussion section at the end of it.

Children who are carers

It is estimated that 10 000 children under the age of 16 are informal carers (Sandwell, 1989), that they usually provide this care for disabled parents, and most likely in a single parent household.

ACTIVITY 34   ALLOW 15 MINUTES

What special psychological effects might children face when they are providing care for a disabled parent? You may find it helpful to look again at Case Study 1 in Activity 7. Write down your ideas.

Commentary

The most important psychological effect on children who are carers is on their normal child development. Part of normal child and adolescent development involves personal and educational development. The kinds of psychological and developmental problems which arise when children are carers are:

- poor school attendance
- a difficulty in forming social relationships
- isolation.

Children often go unrecognised as carers by service practitioners. Hills (1991) found that children are not expected to be carers and that therefore service providers do not recognise their caring role. Children can also deny that they are taking on the role of carer out of fear of being disloyal to their ill or disabled parent. Some children also deny their caring role because they believe they might be taken away from their parent and into care. In this sense it could be said that children are punished for caring (Aldridge and Becker, 1993).

3: What psychological support is needed by informal carers?

The next part of the session will explore how the psychological needs of carers can be met and how the mixed economy of care can support informal carers.

ACTIVITY 35   ALLOW 15 MINUTES

In your own words, write a summary of the key psychological effects (or potential effects) which might arise for informal carers, whether these carers are adults or children.

Commentary

If you had any difficulty doing this activity, read through the previous section again.

The original Griffiths Report (1988) suggested that choice and efficiency in community care were shown to be stimulated through a 'mixed economy approach' where public, private and voluntary services compete on an equal footing to provide services (Means and Smith, 1994, p. 53). The word 'compete' is highlighted here because people who are competing are in danger of forgetting the needs and contribution of informal carers. Instead let us replace the word compete with the word co-operate.

This is suggested because there is evidence to show that the stress experienced by informal carers means that all those involved in community care need to adopt an educative/supportive model in their interactions with these carers. The article you read by Nolan et al., (1990) highlights this. Furthermore, we suggest that if all agencies in the mixed economy of care are to take on a role in support of the informal carer (to relieve their stress and thus enable them to continue in their caring role), all agencies providing community care must have detailed knowledge of the carer/dependant relationship.

Nolan et al., (1990) suggest that the agencies will only gain detailed knowledge if there is a high degree of trust between carer, dependant and the community care service providers. They also suggest that this trust will only develop where there is a sharing of caring tasks and regular contact between all parties. This relies on co-operation within the mixed economy of care rather than competition.

Regular contact between all parties includes carer, dependant, nursing service, voluntary sector, social services and relevant private sector agencies and means collaboration rather than competition. One of the positive outcomes of this collaboration is relief of carer stress.

In the absence of a clear indication of the specific factors which increase stress in carers, Parker (1992) suggests that a more useful approach may be to think about the factors which help carers to cope. She highlights the following factors which increase carers' ability to cope:

- time off from caring
- satisfaction with the help they receive from others
- receiving services.

We will look at each of these in more detail.

Time off from caring

ACTIVITY 36   ALLOW **15** MINUTES

What do you think 'time off from caring' means? Give specific examples.

Commentary ·

Many professionals perceive 'time off from caring' to mean the same thing as the dependent person going somewhere else to be cared for, for a short time. But this is only one aspect of the idea.

Parker (1992) suggests that one of the most significant factors in relieving stress in informal carers might be time away from the dependant. This may be through the carer's getting out for a while or because the dependent person can. Levin et al.,(1989) found that this applied to carers of the elderly as much as it does to those who care for children or young adults.

Other studies have demonstrated that if mothers of disabled children are able to go out to work, this offers strong protection for them against the stress of being a carer.

Although time off from caring is seen as a powerful way of relieving carer stress, most studies show that only two per cent of carers who were helping a dependant in the same household had time off through the dependant's being able to spend some time away from the home (Twigg, 1992).

Fewer than one third of young adult or child dependants attended school, college, work or organised social activities to enable them to get out of the home and thus give their carers time off. Of spouses who were carers for their husbands or wives 70 per cent are unlikely to have had a break of two days since becoming a carer.

Another way of taking time off from caring is when the carer can get away from the house to go to some activity away from home.

ACTIVITY 37 ALLOW 15 MINUTES

Give two or three examples of activities outside the home which carers might do to enable them to have some time off. Can you think of the reasons why this helps reduce stress? Write down your suggestions.

Activities carers might do outside the home:

Reasons why this may help reduce stress:

Commentary

Your suggestions might have included:

- paid work
- education/training course
- social/sporting activity.

Activities such as these relieve stress for carers by offering:

- social interaction
- relief from loneliness and isolation
- mental stimulation
- respite from the physical activities of caring and self-esteem.

However, among all carers, the research shows that half had no day-time activity which would take them out of the home. For those carers who were heavily involved in personal and/or physical tasks of caring, the percentage is nearly 60 per cent. In addition, the more heavily involved carers were in personal/physical caring tasks, the less likely they were to have a paid job to enable them to get out.

Satisfaction about help from others

The second factor which increases carers' ability to cope is the satisfaction they feel about the help they get from others.

There is no substantive evidence that the *amount of help* given by other informal helpers reduces the stress in carers. But there is evidence that it is the extent to which carers are *happy* with the help they get which makes a difference (Gilhooly, 1986). Help from others is not only about physical care and practical help. Such help also offers the opportunity for intimacy; a person to talk to and confide in and emotional support. Parker (1992) found that caring for a disabled spouse reduces the carers' social networks and that any intervention from others, including voluntary organisations, will assist in maintaining those networks.

Provision of services for carers

The third factor which helps carers to cope is related to the services provided specifically for them. Twigg (1992) points out that carers often fall through the net of service provision because they are neither patients nor clients. She identifies these services for carers:

- specific carer services

- carer allocations.

Specific carer services

These are services which are completely geared to carers. They have the word 'carer' or 'relative' in the title and are most often found in the voluntary sector. Some mainstream private and public agencies, such as respite care, also come into this category.

Although they tend to be small in scale, specific carer services are perceived as central in the support for informal carers. On a national level, the Carers' National Association provides specific carer services (information, advice, support and networks with other carers). The association also functions as a charitable pressure group to bring the needs and problems of the carer to the attention of government and the media.

Carer allocations

Services to carers also include the help from primarily statutory (public) agencies, geared to the dependent person but which serve the needs of the carer as well. These services include, for example, day-care services for the elderly to provide relief for the carer. Providing a service for the cared-for person also provides a service for the carer.

Use of paid and unpaid volunteers is a way in which the private and voluntary sectors can provide a service to carers.

Service assumptions and practices

Parker (1992) offers this as a third service for carers. Service assumptions and practices are about how the public sector care providers (doctors, nurses, ambulance personnel) can change their assumptions to take carers' needs into account . Parker argues that changing the assumptions we have about carers and what they are available to do can be the most supportive aspect of care for them.

Activity 38 will help you to identify the kinds of assumptions which formal carers tend to make about informal carers.

ACTIVITY 38   ALLOW 15 MINUTES

From your experience, what assumptions do you think doctors, nurses (and other service providers) make about informal carers? Write down your ideas.

Commentary

Service providers often make certain assumptions about carers. Examples are:

● assuming relatives are available to provide care on discharge from hospital

● assuming that certain care tasks or duties can or will be done by carers

● assuming that carers can, do or wish to have a high degree of involvement in providing informal care.

Practical examples of these assumptions include nurses/doctors who:

● assume that because a daughter is living with an elderly person she can/wishes to/is available to care for the dependent relative

● assume that ambulances can be ordered to arrive at any time because the carer will always be available at that time

● assume that patients can be discharged at any time and that a carer will be available when the patient arrives home.

4: Support services, groups and networks in a mixed economy of care

Caring is not, as is sometimes assumed, merely a public sector issue with some involvement by the voluntary sector. As you saw in Session Two, historically the health service focused on acute, hospital-based care, and this led health service professionals to believe that informal carers were not of central concern to their work and responsibilities.

The change in emphasis to community-based care, however, has led to an increased recognition of the role that informal carers play and the need to provide support.

Community-based health care agencies have traditionally been the main source of contact for informal carers. Community-based professionals who have a great deal of awareness and sensitivity to the needs of carers, recognise and meet these needs fairly well.

The mixed economy of care indicates that care for the ill or disabled person can be carried out through co-operation, as well as through competition, between the health service, voluntary sector, social services and independent sector. However, problems arise in providing support for carers because they occupy an ambiguous position within the care system (Twigg, 1992).

Public and independent health care organisations could provide better support to carers if they understood how their organisations could relate to carers. This involves identifying how carers can best be used. Twigg (1989) offers four models to explain how organisations can relate to carers. These are:

- viewing carers as resources
- viewing carers as co-workers
- viewing carers as co-clients
- viewing carers as superseded carers.

ACTIVITY 39   ALLOW 1 HOUR

Read Twigg (1989) Models of Carers: how do social care agencies conceptualise their relationship with informal carers? *Resource 2* in the *Resources Section.*

Briefly summarise in your own words the four models as described by Twigg. Give examples and possible problems, especially with regard to the support each model might or might not offer to the carer.

	What it means	Examples and problems
Carers as resources		
Carers as co-workers		
Carers as co-clients		
Superseded carers		

Commentary

Carers as resources

Twigg identifies this as the prevailing reality of community care, in which the majority of help that comes to the cared-for comes from informal carers. Public and independent sector agencies who work in this model regard informal care as the first line of care and therefore only see the need to provide care when informal care is unavailable.

In this model the client is the central focus and the carer is the key resource. Healthcare agencies do not see they have a responsibility to be involved in issues related to the welfare of carers, and agencies also do not recognise any potential for conflict between carer and client. Public service agencies who work in this model are often worried that there will be a need for formal care services to substitute for informal care provision. Agencies who work in this model also make assumptions about the availability of the carer to provide care.

Carers as co-workers
This is a totally different philosophy where the care agency (private, public or voluntary) aims to work alongside informal carers. The concept of co-operation is central to this model. Informal care and formal care, whether independent or public sector, are interwoven. As such, although the primary focus remains with the client, the agency regards the morale of the carer and the support required as being important and sees that the continuation and quality of care relies on the carer being supported.

There can be a conflict between the needs of the carer and the needs of the dependent person, but the needs of the dependant are seen as the priority.

Carers as co-clients
This model employs a philosophy where carers are seen as needing help and support in their own right separate from the needs of the client. Agencies who employ this model of support for carers provide services to carers which are specifically designed to relieve their situation and enhance their morale. However, agencies which use this model to support carers have a limited definition of carer. In this model, carers are only those who are exceptionally heavily burdened or deeply stressed and support is geared to this group of carers only.

This model recognises that there is an inherent conflict of interest between the client and carer, and the primary emphasis is placed on the problems which these conflicts cause for the carer, and how these can be resolved in the carer's best interests.

Superseded carers
This is a more complex model of care support. Agencies who use this model to provide support to informal carers do so in an attempt to transcend the care-giving relationship. There are two ways of working using this model. The first is by starting with the aim of maximising the cared-for person's independence, so that the disabled person can be freed from dependence on the carer. This model has been particularly relevant for adults with learning disabilities and their relationship with their carer.

The second way of using this model in practice begins with a concern for the carer. Again, the aim is to maximise independence on the part of the disabled person, but the reason for doing this is to ease the burden of the carer. Agencies who use this model often support the carer in the decision to stop being carer.

Agencies who use either route of this model often deliberately do not use the word 'carer' at all because it is fraught with implied moral responsibility. Instead a word like 'relative' is used because it is perceived more neutrally. The focus of intervention may be on either the carer or the cared-for person. However, either way the carer and cared-for person are seen separately and the valued outcome is independence for both parties, regardless of the route.

Summary

1 You have focused on who informal carers are and what they do and explored some of the positive and negative psychological effects of being an informal carer. A sliding scale of involvement in care from heavy to superficial or light involvement has been identified. Negative psychological effects on the carer can result from feelings of entrapment leading to emotional exhaustion, loneliness and depression. Positive psychological

effects experienced by the carer can include feelings of well-being and increased self-esteem.

2   You have explored the nature of psychological support for carers and the different approaches to informal carer support. This support was considered within the context of a mixed economy of care. There is a school of thought that suggests informal carers may fall through the net, particularly when multi-agency care strategies are employed.

Before you move on to Session Six, check that you have achieved the objectives given at the beginning of this session and, if not, review the appropriate sections.

SESSION SIX

Voluntary groups and psychological needs

Introduction

The role of voluntary groups has expanded in recent years. We explored the reasons for this in Session Two. You should at this stage review the work you did in that session, paying particular attention to the sections dealing with voluntary groups. In this session we will explore the importance of voluntary groups in the mixed economy of care from the following perspectives:

- the culture and roles of these groups

- the roles of volunteers within them

- why individuals join and belong to voluntary groups.

Session objectives

When you have completed this session you should be able to:

- give examples of the range of activities voluntary groups provide

- critically examine the role of individuals in shaping group philosophy and psychology

- identify and examine the needs voluntary groups meet for their members

- discuss the implications of the psychological contract for individuals and groups

- critically explore the impact of the mixed economy of care on the voluntary sector.

1: The culture and role of voluntary groups

The voluntary sector and the private or commercial sector make up the independent sector. These two, together with the statutory sector, make up the mixed economy of care.

In Session Two we looked at the recent shift in provision of care from the statutory sector to the independent sector. This is tied up with:

- the introduction of a market culture to health and social welfare

- a belief that innovation and best practice are to be found in the independent sector

- attempts to be more flexible in approach

- attempts to be more innovative in service delivery

- a search for a more efficient way of delivering services

- the introduction of choice.

ACTIVITY 40   ALLOW 10 MINUTES

Can you suggest why the mixed economy of care may lead to changes in the voluntary sector itself? Write down your suggestions.

Commentary

For voluntary organisations the mixed economy of care means that

- they are now providers of direct services

- they may become dependent on statutory contracts

- their advocacy role is undermined

- they can no longer campaign for improvements in services.

Part of the role of the voluntary sector has been to challenge the complacency of the statutory and independent or commercial sectors. The voluntary sector has traditionally campaigned for the rights of the individuals it represents. But with the move of the voluntary sector into the mixed economy of care, voluntary organisations are losing their original focus. They are less able to represent the views of their members.

ACTIVITY 41   ALLOW 5 MINUTES

Consider the nature of voluntary work and list some of the caring activities performed by voluntary organisations on behalf of those they represent.

Commentary

Among the activities voluntary groups undertake are:

- resource provision e.g. aids to independent living

- provision of information

- befriending

- advocacy

- public education

- campaigning

- innovation

- monitoring.

Not all voluntary groups will engage in all of these activities; some will choose to specialise. But many of these activities will be placed in jeopardy if voluntary groups enter the market economy and become paid providers of services.

The intention of the Community Care Act was to increase the voluntary sector's responsibility to influence the shape and content of community care provisions at planning level (Griffiths, 1988). The introduction of contracting has driven voluntary groups to become competitive bidders for contracts to care, thus putting at risk many of their original declared intentions (Handy, 1988).

ACTIVITY 42

Handy (1988) identifies five categories of voluntary organisation, although a voluntary group often falls into more than one category. They are:

- service providers
- research and advocacy
- support and assistance
- common interest or enthusiasm
- intermediary bodies who provide help, skills and advice on policy.

Think of the local and national voluntary agencies you know about. Talk to colleagues to get more ideas if you need to. List the organisations under the appropriate categories.

Service providers

Research and advocacy

Support and assistance

Common interest or enthusiasm

Help, skills and advice on policy.

Commentary

You may have found that many organisations will carry out a number of functions. Some examples are the following:

- Dr Barnados provides services
- The Child Poverty Action Group and SCOPE carry out research and advocacy
- Alcoholics Anonymous offers support and assistance to alcoholics
- groups such as the National Food Allowance Alliance bring members together round a common theme and interest – that of food and poverty.

The activities and purpose of a voluntary group reflect its culture and group psychology. But the individuals that make up the group and society at large will also influence a group's culture and purpose. The relationship between the group culture and the people who belong to the group is one of interdependence – as one changes, the other is likely to change as well. This is why the activities of voluntary groups can tell you a lot about the psychology of the group and also of the individuals who belong to it.

2: The roles volunteers play

Individuals join groups in order to have their needs met. As Handy (1988) notes, this involves a psychological balancing act between what individuals are able to contribute to a voluntary organisation and what they are able to gain from being a member.

There are different types of voluntary organisation just as there are a variety of volunteers performing various roles. Think back to Session Four and role casting. This concept will be used here to explore the roles found in groups. You may find it helpful to re-read sections 1 to 5 of Session Four before you continue.

Belbin's teams

Belbin (1981) has made a long study of the best mix of personal characteristics in a group, starting with his discovery of the Apollo syndrome – the finding that a team composed of the brightest people did not necessarily or even often end up as the brightest and the best. He listed eight roles which are needed in a group. One person can sometimes do two but rarely more roles. He argued that a group which does not have someone carrying out each of these roles will perform below its best on most complex tasks or problems. The roles are:

- the chairman – the co-ordinator. Disciplined, focused and balanced rather than brilliant or creative, he or she is a good listener and a good judge.

- the shaper – the task leader. Full of drive, achievement and passion, he or she can be oversensitive and irritable but provides the spur to action.

- the plant – the ideas person. Introverted and quiet but intellectually dominant. Sensitive and easily hurt, he or she can also be careless of detail and may switch off.

- the monitor – the evaluator – the critic. He or she has the ability to see the flaw in the argument, is analytically intelligent and often slightly less involved than others.

- the resource investigator – the popular extrovert. The sales person, diplomat or liaison officer brings new contacts and ideas to the group although he or she doesn't do much with them personally.

- the company worker – the practical organiser. He or she turns ideas into tasks, schedules and plans, an administrator rather than a leader.

- the team worker – the building force. He or she is uncompetitive but committed, likeable, good at listening and good at building bridges between other people.

- the finisher – the one who worries about deadlines and completion of tasks. Without this individual tasks might never be finished as other members of the team will keep refining and adding to the task.

ACTIVITY 43   ALLOW 45 MINUTES

This is a reflective activity, asking you to apply these roles to your own experience. Think of a group you are involved in at work or in a voluntary capacity. Identify the roles played by individuals in the group you are thinking of. What roles do you perform?

Group:	Who plays the role?	Roles I play (tick)
Chairman		
The shaper		
The plant		
The monitor		
The resource investigator		
The company worker		
The team worker		
The finisher		

Commentary

Bear in mind that individuals can play more than one role in a group. The contribution that individuals make helps the group to achieve its purpose and functions. The roles are a mixture of task and maintenance roles. Task roles are those such as the chairman, the company worker and the finisher. These are focused on the tasks being accomplished. The maintenance roles, such as the resource investigator and the team worker, contribute to the emotional life of the group.

Both categories are necessary for the group to be successful. Task roles can lead to a task being accomplished but if no emotional life is fostered volunteers will not come back for more.

You might have found it hard to identify the roles you play; if you did, tick the ones with which you feel most comfortable. You may find it helpful to discuss the roles you have ticked with a friend or colleague to find out their impression of the roles you perform.

Roles in groups

The roles we play are based on two major influences: our own expectations and the expectations others have of us. The group philosophy in voluntary groups is generally concerned with doing good and helping others. This means that very often members of voluntary groups cannot say no. They keep taking on extra work. This leads to what is known as the 'servant syndrome' (Handy, 1988). It is a common feature of charities and voluntary groups. The servant syndrome is also true of carers and may result in health problems – either psychological or physical. It is not clear whether voluntary groups attract members with a 'servant syndrome' psychological profile or whether the psychological impetus of the group is imposed on members.

3: Why do people join voluntary groups?

ACTIVITY 44   ALLOW 15 MINUTES

Make a list of the reasons why you think people join voluntary groups. Draw on your own experience of groups.

Commentary

There are many reasons. Some of them are:

- for company
- to help others
- to be useful
- for an activity
- for support
- to use existing skills
- to belong
- religious belief
- belief in doing good
- helping those less fortunate than themselves
- because of feelings of anger.

Notice that some of these reasons relate to individuals receiving feedback which has an impact on their psychological profile. Support is important to many people in voluntary groups. The sharing of problems does not change their circumstances but it may help to influence their perception of their situation. Knowing there are others in similar circumstances reduces feelings of loneliness and isolation.

Different personality types will be attracted towards different groups and activities. It is important to note that it is not just that we are attracted to environments and organisations which suit our psychological profile. We also seek out those areas or environments which help us to be what we would like to be.

Holland (1973) identified six environments:

- realistic
- intellectual
- social
- conventional
- enterprising
- artistic.

Let's look at how different environments and character traits may match up.

ACTIVITY 45 　　　　　　ALLOW 15 MINUTES

Consider the environments listed above. What types of people – in terms of character traits – may be attracted to each one? What kind of activities would such people enjoy? Note down your ideas.

Environment	Type of person likely to be attracted to this	Activities they may enjoy
Realistic		
Intellectual		
Social		
Conventional		
Enterprising		
Artistic		

Commentary

Here are our suggestions, which are adapted from Handy (1988):

Environment	Type of person likely to be attracted to this	Activities they may enjoy
Realistic	People who seek objective, concrete goals and tasks and like to manipulate things.	Such people are best suited to outdoor work and practical jobs.
Intellectual	People for whom ideas, words and symbols are important.	They are best suited to tasks requiring abstract and creative abilities. They are likely to be leaders and innovators in a group, but not necessarily the hands-on type.
Social	People who are interested in other people and have good interpersonal skills.	They are likely to be involved in counselling, support work and fund raising.

Conventional	People who like rules and boundaries are attracted to this environment.	The tasks they will enjoy include office work and administration.
Enterprising	High energy, enthusiastic, dominating and extrovert people look to this environment.	They are likely to be involved in advocacy, policy formation, campaigning and setting up services.
Artistic	People who like using intuition and feeling, imagination.	They may be involved in counselling and campaigning activities.

Volunteers can play different roles in different types of organisations. In some they are the core professionals (as in marriage guidance groups). In some they occupy the dual roles of clients and providers. Many members of carer support groups fit this scenario.

Membership of any group involves both give and take. This is sometimes called the psychological contract. It is like a see-saw: members of voluntary groups give their time, skills and energy and in return something is given to them. This is usually in the form of psychological strokes which make people feel rewarded and boost their self-esteem.

We have seen the interdependence between individuals who join and make up voluntary groups and the psychology and culture of the groups themselves. Thus we can see that changes in voluntary groups will affect their members.

4: Effects of the mixed economy of care

The recent development in the mixed economy of care in turning voluntary groups into pseudo-statutory services may conflict with the roles of voluntary groups and the roles of individuals within them. The current changes in voluntary groups are indicative of the pressures they are facing from the outside world.

Change is not necessarily good or bad and it remains to be seen whether the changes and the introduction of the mixed economy of care will have negative influences on groups and voluntary bodies which engage in support for carers. What is clear is that the changes related to the mixed economy of care will bring about changes within these groups. By being aware of change we are able to be proactive in helping to shape the changes.

What is known is that the 'fight or flight' syndrome is common in individuals and groups who are under pressure. The tendency to engage in displacement activities such as fighting with one another or running away does not solve the problem; instead it distracts attention away from it.

Many voluntary groups faced with the changes created by the mixed economy of care may deal with their pressure by 'fight or flight'. If we recognise what is happening we are in a position to influence it.

The following quote by Handy (1988) describes the effects of the current developments in the mixed economy of care.

'Many voluntary organisations have found themselves becoming the agents of their paymasters, be those paymasters a government department, a local authority or the Manpower Services Commission.'

ACTIVITY 46 — ALLOW 10 MINUTES

Make a list of the consequences of the changes created by the mixed economy of care for a voluntary group.

Commentary

Among the consequences you may have noted are the following:

- change in philosophy and outlook
- change in function
- change in membership and recruitment
- become service provider
- less able to act as advocate on behalf of members
- less able to campaign.

The changes in the mixed economy of care and the development of a market economy in the health and social welfare provision have led to voluntary groups competing with each other and the commercial and statutory sectors (Ellert, 1995).

The future for voluntary groups is unclear. The introduction of the mixed economy of care is in its early stages of development and the full impact has yet to be felt.

Summary

1 We have explored the culture and role of voluntary groups within the mixed economy of care. There is a place for such groups, particularly as statutory resources are finite. Individuals and groups are seen to be interdependent in shaping corporate and individual psychology towards a particular style of caring.

2 There is a range of roles and environments within voluntary groups and in the attraction of these to people with different personalities or psychological profiles.

3 Two categories of role exist: (a) those concerned with maintenance of tasks and (b) those concerned with achievement of tasks.

4 Groups deal with pressure in terms of standing to fight or backing off. This merely serves to divert and occupy groups without actually solving the problem.

Before you move on to Session Seven, check that you have achieved the objectives given at the beginning of this session and, if not, review the appropriate sections.

SESSION SEVEN

Towards healthy caring relationships

Introduction

In this session we shall examine the concept of a healthy caring relationship, what it means, how it can be achieved and the role of the agencies within the mixed economy of care in promoting and sustaining healthy caring relationships.

Before beginning this session, review Session Two as this forms the building blocks for this session.

Session objectives

When you have completed this session you should be able to:

- define and discuss in depth what is meant by a healthy caring relationship

- use an interactionist model to explore caring relationships

- discuss the conditions within the interactionist model which enable a caring relationship to be a healthy one

- identify the ways in which agencies and organisations within the mixed economy of care can contribute to healthy caring relationships.

1: What is a healthy caring relationship?

Defining what is meant by a healthy caring relationship requires some clarification of the three words. Not all health-related relationships are caring relationships and not all caring relationships are necessarily healthy caring relationships.

In Session One you had the opportunity to examine what caring means from a number of perspectives.

The word 'healthy' seems to have a positive value attached to it. It implies something which is good, desired, valued, enriching and fulfilling, as opposed to its opposite word, 'unhealthy', which has a negative value attached to it. The word healthy has as its root word, 'heal'.

ACTIVITY 47 — ALLOW 30 MINUTES

This is a reflective activity. It involves thinking through each question and only writing something down after you've thought it through. The thinking and feeling part of the activity is what is most important; the writing part is merely to enable you to remember what you have thought and felt.

1 What does the word 'heal' mean to you? What feelings does it bring for you. Write down your thoughts and feelings.

2 How does the way you defined 'heal' influence your understanding of the word 'healthy'? Write down your own understanding of the word 'healthy'.

Commentary

You may have used words like 'cure' or 'therapeutic' or 'to make better' as your definition of heal. Perhaps you discussed healing in physical, psychological and spiritual contexts. Let us look at one particular approach to health in a healthy relationship.

Jourard (1971) suggested that a healing relationship is one which serves to increase the individual's sense of purpose, integrity and identity. It is a relationship in which each person feels valued as an individual, and offers and receives understanding and empathy from the other.

What this seems to suggest is that a healing relationship may also be a healthy relationship because feeling understood, having a sense of purpose and individuality, having a sense of personal integrity and personal identity, are all components of health.

It seems logical that the goal of all people involved in the mixed economy of care is a healing relationship. A healing, caring relationship is also a healthy caring relationship.

2: A model for a healthy caring relationship

Ultimately, we are interested in a caring relationship which is a healthy one. In Session Three we described three perspectives which contributed to the psychology of care given by informal carers. These three perspectives are:

- the caring role (behaviours)

- the psychology of the carer

- the responsibilities of the carer.

These three perspectives offer different understandings of the psychology of care and yet, at the same time, there is an overlap between them. The three perspectives can, therefore, be represented by the interactionist model shown in *Figure 19*.

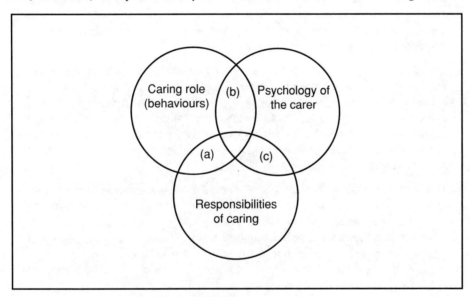

Figure 19 : The interactionist model (1)

You will notice that areas of overlap in *Figure 19* have been labelled with the letters a, b and c. We will explore these three areas of overlap in the following activity.

ACTIVITY 48 ALLOW 30 MINUTES

To consider the following questions you may find it helpful to review your work on Session Three.

1 Look at the overlap between the caring role and responsibilities of caring. How might you label and describe the overlap area marked with the letter 'a' in *Figure 19*?

2 How might you label and describe the overlap area marked with a letter 'b' in *Figure 19*?

3. How might you label and describe the area of overlap marked with a letter 'c' in *Figure 19*?

Commentary

In Session Three we suggested that, in psychological terms, the caring role is dependent upon both the needs of the person being cared for and the abilities of the carer. We discussed this further in Session Five. The case studies you examined in Session Three demonstrated the needs of dependants versus the abilities of carers. When you looked at the responsibilities of caring in Session Three, you examined more than just physical responsibilities of care and looked at emotional, power and support issues.

When examining the interaction area marked with the letter 'a' in *Figure 20*, then, we are in essence looking at the personal limitations of caring. It is this that represents the common area where the caring role interacts with the responsibilities of the carer. These limitations to caring might be due to the age of the carer, the relationship between the carer and dependant, the gender of the carer, available resources, emotional issues, power issues and the amount of support available to the carer.

The area of interaction at point 'b' in *Figure 19* is the area where the caring role and the psychology of the carer interact with each other. The psychology of the carer influences the attitudes towards the caring role. In psychological terms, what is of primary importance is how the attitude towards the caring role is perceived by the carer (and by the dependant and formal carers). This area of interaction between the caring role and the psychology of the carer can be labelled at point 'b' as the perceptions of attitude to the caring role.

Finally, at point 'c' in *Figure 19* we see where the psychology of the carer interacts with the responsibilities of the carer. This is where perception and responsibilities come together and could be described as perceptions of the limitations of caring responsibilities.

You may have used different words to describe the overlapping or interacting areas at points a, b and c, but regardless of the way you described and labelled your diagram you should have come up with similar relationships between the overlapping components. *Figure 20* shows the interactionist model with the areas of overlap identified.

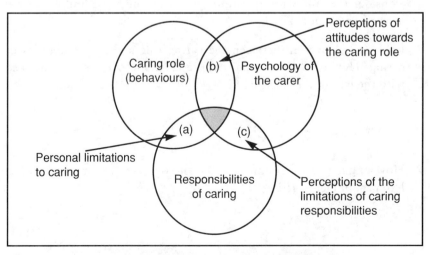

Figure 20: The interactionist model (2)

Limitations, misperceptions and shared perceptions

The word 'limitations' has a negative connotation. It focuses on what we are unable to do rather than on that which we feel we ought to do or wish to do. *Figure 21* highlights two areas of interaction that create points of limitation in care. Identifying limitations, however, is about how reality (or our perceptions of reality) influences the ideal. Identifying limitations is the first step to accepting limitations, and accepting limitations is part of a healthy caring relationship.

When carers – both formal and informal – do not recognise and accept their limitations, they try to achieve an ideal which is impossible and feel guilty for not doing so. This increases stress in the carer. Limitations are legitimate realities in caring. They enable us to set realistic expectations and targets that we can meet.

An unhealthy caring relationship, then, is where the carer and the cared for fail to recognise the limitations of caring and the limitations of caring responsibilities. Similarly, an unhealthy caring relationship can occur when perceptions of attitudes towards the caring role are either unrealistic or do not match up between carer and dependant or between informal carer and formal care agencies. Misperceptions of attitudes and responsibilities lead to false or unshared assumptions about the carer, the caring role and the responsibilities of the carer.

3: Towards healthy caring relationships

ACTIVITY 49 — ALLOW 5 MINUTES

The interactionist model attempts to explain how a healthy caring relationship can be created through understanding the relationship between caring roles, the psychology of the carer and the responsibilities of the carer. When the interaction between the parts – between carer, dependant and agency – works, the result is a healthy caring relationship.

If you look again at *Figure 20*, you will see a shaded area in the middle of the model where all three circles come together.

How might you label or describe this shaded area of interaction?

Commentary

The shaded area represents the healthy caring relationship. In order for a healthy caring relationship to exist, the following must happen:

● carers must have the opportunity to explore and examine the caring role and the nature of the responsibilities of a carer

● carers need to identify, understand, articulate and accept their personal limitations in their particular caring role

● carers need support from agencies within the mixed economy of care based on accurate, shared perceptions between carer and agencies so that formal care is targeted to real needs.

A healthy caring relationship can only exist if the above are in place.

ACTIVITY 50   ALLOW 30 MINUTES

The chart below identifies the important parts of the interactionist model. Fill in the boxes indicating what needs to happen in order to create a healthy caring relationship with regard to each part of the model. You may wish to refer back to previous activities in this session or to Sessions Three and Five.

What would make the caring relationship a healthy one?	
Caring role (behaviours)	
Psychology of the carer	
Responsibilities of the carer	
Personal limitations of the carer	
Perceptions of limitations of caring responsibilities	
Perceptions of attitudes towards the caring role	

Commentary

Here are our suggestions.

- The extent to which a carer is able to undertake the caring role required. This may be influenced by the age of the carer, gender, physical limitations of the carer and resources available.

- The extent to which the carer's role takes up the carer's life. Support, opportunities for respite care and opportunities for social interaction outside the home all affect the attitude the carer has towards the caring role.

- The extent to which the needs of the dependant can be met; the extent to which the carer feels empowered or disempowered in the caring role, and the extent to which carers perceive they are in control of their own lives.

- The extent to which the carer's limitations are understood, perceived and recognised in an non-judgemental way by formal care agencies.

- The provision of appropriate support from agencies to provide care when the carer's limitations have been identified.

- The extent to which all the limitations, expectations and perceptions are articulated and shared between carer, dependant and formal care agency.

In summary, limitations to care become positive when they are recognised in a non-judgemental way and are accepted and understood by dependants and formal carers so that appropriate support and help can be offered. When perceptions of expectations, roles and responsibilities are shared, misperceptions and unrealistic expectations are avoided.

Carers are not to blame for caring limitations. Given the high number of informal carers who provide the major amount of care to a dependent person at home, the public, independent and voluntary agencies need to identify ways of contributing to healthy caring relationships.

4: How can community care agencies contribute to healthy caring relationships?

Community care agencies are agencies within the mixed economy of care. They include those in the public sector (e.g. social services, housing authorities, community trusts, purchasers or commissioners of services); those in the independent sector (e.g. private residential and housing agencies and domestic service agencies); and those in the voluntary sector (for example, charities, self-help organisations, pressure groups, clubs and care attendant schemes).

Apart from the practical help which these groups provide – either in competition with each other or in partnership/collaboration with each other – there is much that they can contribute to creating healthy caring relationships.

Robinson (1988) suggested that although society has to place responsibility for care with the dependants' families, society must also recognise that there are limits to the responsibilities which families can be expected to bear. So in the sector of the interactionist model called responsibilities of the carer, care agencies need to recognise that as well as responsibilities, carers also have rights. It is the responsibility of caring agencies to identify these rights, respect them and provide appropriate support to enable carers' rights to be maintained.

ACTIVITY 51

1 What is a right?

2 Draw up a list of the rights you think carers should reasonably expect to have.

Commentary

Perhaps you will agree that a right is what constitutes fair treatment or justice. The Social Work Services Group (1984) identified six carers' rights. They are:

- time off to themselves
- to be consulted in policy matters
- some priority in services
- training in caring
- counselling
- to choose the model of carer best suited to their needs.

How do these rights compare with your list?

From these rights, many authors (Corbin and Strauss, 1988; Robinson, 1988) have identified some basic needs of carers. These are:

- information on topics ranging from details of their dependant's illness and treatment to details about the availability of services. Carers need information to make informed choices to enable them to exercise some control over the services they require

- skills training in nursing care, dealing with specific problems (for example, incontinence) and specific techniques (for example, lifting)

- emotional support ranging from recognition of the value of their work and having someone to talk to, to dealing with the range of emotions experienced (for example, guilt, depression, helplessness), to setting boundaries to their role and responsibility

- regular respite from their role as a carer.

When these needs are met, there is a healthy caring relationship between carer and dependant. When these needs are met as a result of planned, well co-ordinated, co-operative provision by the agencies within the mixed economy of care, then the healthy caring relationship is a *tri-partite* healthy caring relationship between carer, dependant and agencies.

Having examined how the agencies within a mixed economy of care can contribute to a healthy relationship, it will be useful for you to consider how you, as a formal carer, can contribute to a healthy caring relationship.

ACTIVITY 52	ALLOW 20 MINUTES

Consider how you, in your role as a formal carer, can contribute to a healthy caring relationship by looking at each part of the interactionist model. Write your ideas under each of the areas in the interactionist model: caring role, psychology of carer and so on.

Component parts of interactionist model	How can you in your professional role help/contribute?
Caring role	
Psychology of the carer	
Responsibilities of the carer	
Personal limitations of the carer	
Perceptions of limitations of caring responsibilities	
Perceptions of attitudes towards the caring role	

Commentary

There are no right or wrong answers to offer. Instead, perhaps you might talk to your colleagues and share ideas about how individuals can contribute to creating healthy caring relationships between formal carers, informal carers, agencies, organisations and patients/clients.

Summary

1 This session has defined the healthy caring relationship by exploring the three words: health, caring and relationship.

2 We have devised an interactionist model to enable you to examine what influences a healthy caring relationship and how such a relationship can be created.

Now that you have completed Session Seven you should have a clear idea of how all the organisations within the mixed economy of care and individual informal carers can contribute to healthy caring relationships. If not, review the appropriate sections. You can then go on to complete the learning review that follows this session.

LEARNING REVIEW

Now that you have completed your work on this unit, you may like to assess your progress and understanding. You can do this by completing the following learning review, and comparing your responses with those you gave before you started Session One.

	Not at all	Partly	Quite well	Very well

Session One

I can:

- give examples of different forms of caring ☐ ☐ ☐ ☐
- discuss what constitutes quality care ☐ ☐ ☐ ☐
- distinguish between the different categories of care ☐ ☐ ☐ ☐
- begin to recognise aspects of psychology and how these relate to providing care. ☐ ☐ ☐ ☐

Session Two

I can:

- give examples of changes in care ☐ ☐ ☐ ☐
- relate improvements in the physical and social environment to changing ways of providing care ☐ ☐ ☐ ☐
- critically discuss some of the myths underlying the provision of care in the community ☐ ☐ ☐ ☐
- give examples of the various organisations which make up the voluntary, independent and statutory sectors ☐ ☐ ☐ ☐
- critically examine and provide reasons for the growth of the informal sector ☐ ☐ ☐ ☐
- explain how social pressures influence carers and their behaviour. ☐ ☐ ☐ ☐

	Not at all	Partly	Quite well	Very well

Session Three

I can:

- critically examine and give examples of factors that influence the psychology of the carer · □ □ □ □
- critically examine and give examples of factors that influence the psychology of the caring role · □ □ □ □
- critically examine and give examples of factors that influence the responsibilities of the carer · □ □ □ □
- discuss and give examples of interactions between these three elements. · □ □ □ □

Session Four

I can:

- critically examine and give examples of role development and role casting · □ □ □ □
- give examples of the usefulness of roles in the caring relationship · □ □ □ □
- critically examine the positive and negative strokes and feedback that carers receive · □ □ □ □
- give examples of the negative aspects of role casting or occupation in formal and informal care settings · □ □ □ □
- discuss critically the interrelationships between various roles in the caring situation · □ □ □ □
- critically examine role relationships between formal and informal carers · □ □ □ □
- reflect on the problems in role relationship between formal and informal carers and conflicts with regard to who the client is. · □ □ □ □

Session Five

I can:

- identify who informal carers are and critically analyse what kinds of care they give · □ □ □ □
- describe the psychological impact of being an informal carer · □ □ □ □

	Not at all	Partly	Quite well	Very well

Session Five *continued*

- describe the kind of psychological support which informal carers may require

| | ☐ | ☐ | ☐ | ☐ |

- give examples of approaches to informal care networks and groups and critically examine the impact these networks have on the psychology of the carer.

| | ☐ | ☐ | ☐ | ☐ |

Session Six

I can:

- critically examine the role of individuals in shaping group philosophy

| | ☐ | ☐ | ☐ | ☐ |

- give examples of the range of activities voluntary groups provide

| | ☐ | ☐ | ☐ | ☐ |

- discuss the implications of the psychological contract for individuals and groups

| | ☐ | ☐ | ☐ | ☐ |

- identify and critically examine the needs which voluntary groups meet for their members

| | ☐ | ☐ | ☐ | ☐ |

- critically explore the impact of the mixed economy of care on the voluntary sector.

| | ☐ | ☐ | ☐ | ☐ |

Session Seven

I can:

- define and discuss in depth what is meant by a healthy caring relationship

| | ☐ | ☐ | ☐ | ☐ |

- use an interactionist model to critically explore caring relationships

| | ☐ | ☐ | ☐ | ☐ |

- discuss the conditions within the interactionist model which enable a caring relationship to be a healthy one

| | ☐ | ☐ | ☐ | ☐ |

- identify ways in which agencies and organisations within the mixed economy of care can contribute to healthy caring relationships.

| | ☐ | ☐ | ☐ | ☐ |

RESOURCES SECTION

Contents

RESOURCE I

Nolan M.R., Grant G.
and Ellis N.C. Journal of
Advanced Nursing 15,
1990

Stress is in the eye of the beholder: reconceptualising the measurement of carer burden

The development of community care policy and the inadequacies of professional responses to the needs of informal carers were described in an earlier paper. A qualitative analysis of carers' replies to a questionnaire survey demonstrated that the most potent stressors, contrary to what has previously been assumed, were linked more to subjective perceptions of events or circumstances than to the objective features of the events and circumstances themselves. This paper presents a quantitative analysis of data from the same survey which confirms the impressions gained from the analysis of the qualitative data. These findings prompt a reconceptualisation of carer burden within a transactional model of stress, which is then considered as a basis for understanding how carers adapt to stress in their lives. Practice implications are assessed.

Introduction

The British government's philosophy of caring for dependency groups in the community and the reification of that policy from care in the community to care by the community has resulted in a burgeoning of research activity in this field. Twigg (1986) in reviewing the research literature on informal carers has identified two main themes: (a) the scope and extent of informal care; and (b) the burdens and costs that caring imposes on those providing care.

Research in the former area has demonstrated quite unequivocally that family members, usually female kin, provide most informal care (Equal Opportunities Commission 1982a,b, Bonny 1984, Henwood & Wicks 1984, Wicks & Henwood 1988) and following the publication of nationally representative data (Green 1988), reliable population estimates of the total number of informal carers are now available. Research in the latter area however has not been so conclusive and, despite an expanding knowledge base, important questions concerning the nature of carer stress and how it might be ameliorated remain unanswered (Parker 1985, Gwyther & George 1986). This paper endeavours to provide some tentative answers to these questions. Previous attempts to conceptualise and measure carer burden are briefly reviewed and it is suggested that they lack a theoretical cohesion and consistency. Using the results from a national sample survey of members of the Association of Carers (now Carers: National Association), carer burden is reconceptualised within a transactional model of stress and an empirical test for such a model is applied. The paper concludes with a consideration of the implications of the results for practice decisions in the field of informal care.

The measurement of carer burden

Research highlighting the vulnerability of informal carers has demonstrated beyond any reasonable doubt that caring often has adverse effects on important domains of carers' lives. Such effects include poor physical and emotional health, impaired social and family life and reduced economic and employment opportunities. Whilst it has been suggested that social and personal life can be highly disrupted (Hooyman et al. 1985, Wright 1986), most of the empirical evidence identifies a deterioration in emotional health as the most prevalent and pervasive consequence of caring (Hirschfield 1981, 1983, Equal Opportunities Commission 1982a, Cantor 1983, Worcester & Quayhagen 1983, Briggs 1983, Bowling 1984, Parker 1985, Brody 1985, Gwyther & George 1986, Bell et al. 1987, Thompson 1987).

However, it is still not clear which factors precipitate these adverse consequences and which carer groups, if any, are the most affected. Dependency factors have been implicated by some (Sandford 1975, Quine & Charnley 1987). On the other hand many studies have failed to identify any clear and consistent relationship between the nature and extent of disability, the duration of caring and the adverse consequences experienced (Fengler & Goodrich 1979, Zarit et al. 1980, Hawranik 1985, Parker 1985, George & Gwyther 1986, Fitting et al. 1986, Winogrond et al. 1987, Eagles et al. 1987, Motenko 1989).

There is a similar confusion about the

effects of caring on different groups. Some authors have considered women to be most at risk (Fitting et al. 1986), others suggest spouses or resident carers irrespective of gender (Cantor 1983, George & Gwyther 1986), whilst still others identify young carers (Hirschfield & Krulick 1985). Furthermore factors considered to ameliorate carer distress differ widely and include the frequency of family visits (Zarit et al. 1980, Hawranik 1985), carer perceived health and the nature of past carer/dependant relationships (Gilleard et al. 1984) and the availability of information and appropriate service interventions (Silverstein 1984, Challis 1985).

Discrepant results such as these undoubtedly reflect in part the diversity of contexts for care. However, the search for common denominators which might help to explain stresses and strains in caring has also been hampered by the small scale and focused nature of much previous work (Parker 1985). All this has been confounded by the failure to apply a consistent theoretical approach to the measurement of carer burden. This paper represents a modest attempt to begin bridging some of these important gaps.

Previous measures of carer burden

Early scaling instruments such as those produced by Zarit et al. (1980) and Robinson (1983) are underpinned by the assumption that the discomforts caused by certain caring tasks or restrictions translate directly to feelings of burden or are stressful in themselves. Furthermore, such instruments often mix, and treat as synonymous, items concerning emotional reactions to caring with those merely seeking to ascertain if certain situations exist in the caring environment. In addition, the summative nature of these tools either assumes the equivalence of stimuli or masks the relative contribution that specific domains of burden make to the overall burden scores. In more recent work the use of factor analytic techniques has overcome some of these problems (Kosberg & Cairl 1986) but the conceptual basis for such scales still assumes that because caring imposes certain restrictions, for example on the social life of carers, then this in itself will be stressful.

The notion of caregiving impact (on family relationships, social life, personal time and employment opportunities) and the degree of strain (on physical and emotional health and finances) as representing separate but related effects marked an important step forward (Cantor 1983). However the fact that impact and degree of strain were used only as dependent variables with no attempt to use impact as a predictor of strain or vice versa appears to limit the utility of these analyses.

Some of the conceptual and methodological confusion apparent in the measurement of carer burden was highlighted by Poulshock & Deimling (1984). In seeking to clarify the issues, they proposed that the term burden be restricted to subjective interpretations of events, preferring the term impact to denote the objective changes in carers' circumstances. A three-stage model was postulated in which burden acted as a mediating influence between levels of impairment in the dependant and the impact on the carer. Thus the model was seen to run in the causal direction:

Impairment → Burden →Impact

Following a series of multivariate analyses these authors contend that impairment in Activities in Daily Living (ADL), mediated via perceived burden, impacts on the carer's social life and that mental impairment, similarly mediated, affects family relationships. The value of this model lies in its recognition of the importance of subject factors in furthering our understanding of carers' problems. Nonetheless, there would appear to be a number of inherent difficulties of a conceptual order.

Firstly, the model is predicated on the assumption that perceived burden is inextricably linked with impairment and the extent of burden is thus confounded with impairment in the measurement process. The authors fall into the conceptual cul-de-sac noted by Zarit & Zarit (1982) of making the inferential leap between levels of impairment and the experience of burden.

Secondly, impact measures on social life and family relationships are treated as 'more or less objective' and no attempt is made to examine their perceived burden.

Furthermore, the impact measures used are unlikely to represent the ultimate consequences of caring and are more likely to be steps along the way to other adverse outcomes, which the empirical evidence already reviewed suggests are most probably manifested in some form of emotional disturbance.

Reconceptualising carer burden

This necessarily perfunctory review of attempts to measure carer burden highlights the areas of conceptual inconsistency which are still apparent. The research on which the remainder of this paper is based places carer burden within a transactional model of stress and applies an empirical test for such an approach.

Seeking to explain one vague concept (burden) in terms of another (stress) might seem like replacing an enigma with a paradox. On the other hand, Clarke (1984a,b) suggests that there is an emerging consensus about the use of concepts of stress as a basis for professional interventions, with the recent literature leaning heavily on the idea of stress as being a transaction between an individual and his or her environment (Hatfield 1987, Spaniol & Jung 1987, Boss 1988, Chilman et al. 1988). Such approaches owe much to the important work of Lazarus (Jacobson 1983) and despite the plethora of current models (Goosen & Bush 1979, Scott et al. 1980, Jacobson 1983, Clarke 1984a,b, Spaniol & Jung 1987), each is underpinned by certain common assumptions. Within such a paradigm it is not the event itself which is important but the individual's perception of the event. 'There's nothing either good or bad but thinking makes it so' (Shakespeare, *Hamlet*). This allows for the possibility of the same event being differentially stress-provoking for different individuals or for the same individual on separate occasions. An appraisal process determines reactions to potentially stressful events in the environment, with stress only resulting when there is a cognitive imbalance between the perceived nature of the demand and the perceived capabilities of the individual concerned.

The foregoing is, of course, a much simplified description of transactional approaches to stress but highlights the central tenet of such models in that it is not the actual but the perceived capabilities and demands that are crucial. If burden is taken to represent the carer's perception of an event then the relevance of transactional definitions of stress to the investigation of burden becomes immediately apparent, as do the limitations of previous models of burden. The advantages of considering carer burden within a wider stress framework were recognised by Zarit et al. (1986), but once again were limited by the failure to account for the differential stress effects of the same stimuli on varying individuals.

The utility of the transactional model in furthering our understanding of carer burden is tested below by the application of multivariate approaches to the analysis of empirical data. The model to be tested runs in the causal direction:

Environment factors→Stress factors → Malaise

'Environment factors' are those to which a carer is exposed within the caring environment and include not only dependency variables, but also social life, financial implications of caring and the relationship between carer and dependant. 'Stress factors' are the carer's subjective appraisal of the degree of discomfort resulting from the environment factors and 'malaise' is the carer's score on a well known measure of stress.

Method

The detailed methodology for the study has been described elsewhere (Nolan & Grant 1989), but in order to place the present

results in context will be briefly rehearsed again. A national sample survey of members of the Association of Carers (now Carers: National Association) was undertaken using a postal questionnaire. The questionnaire comprised the usual details relating to biography, history of the caring relationship, dependency characteristics of the cared-for, together with open questions on the problems and satisfactions of caring. Also included was a previously validated measure of stress (the malaise inventory – Rutter et al. 1970) together with a newly designed instrument, the Carer Perceived Problem Checklist (CPPC). The CPPC contained 30 potential problems carers might face which had been selected following a detailed review of the theoretical and empirical literature. It covered the domains of social life, economic situation, relationship with dependant and the wider family, professional and family support, dependency factors and the carer's reactions to the demands of caregiving. The checklist comprised two sections which asked carers to consider if they experienced a particular stressor in their caring environment and, additionally, to indicate the degree of actual stress they perceived that stressor to provoke.

Questionnaires

Two thousand and fifty questionnaires were forwarded and 726 returned. Of these 554 were subjected to a series of multivariate analyses and 671 to a detailed content analysis. The results of the content analysis have already been described (Nolan & Grant 1989) and they provided a clear indication of the potential utility of the transactional approach to stress in furthering our understanding of carer burden. The results described below are from a complementary quantitative analysis using SPSSX and LISREL VI.

Results

Data were subjected to a series of multivariate analyses including factor analysis and causal path analysis.

Factor analysis

These analyses were carried out using principal components analysis and varimax rotation with the normal default criteria. Three separate analyses were conducted, one on factors in the caring environment, one on the degree of stress that the environment factors were perceived to cause and one on the factor structure of the malaise inventory. From the first of these analyses, 11 factors emerged which have been termed environment factors. These indicate that the carer was exposed to, or experienced, certain combinations of stimuli in their caring environment. These factors, together with their factor loadings, are shown in Table 1. As can be seen, they form highly interpretable clus-ters of variables resulting in empirically meaningful factors.

TABLE 1
Factor structures for caring environment

Factor	Factor loading	Factor	Factor loading
1:*Degree of physical help variable*		5:*Carer's reactions to caring*	
To dress	0.84	Carer can't relax/worried about caring	0.71*
To wash	0.78	Carer feels out of control	0.69*
To toilet	0.76	Carer experiences guilt	0.63*
To mobilise	0.72	Caring threatens emotional health	0.57*
To bathe	0.71	Caring threatens physical health	0.51*
With personal care	0.65*	Caring affects sleep	0.45*
To feed	0.63	Carer feels angry	0.40*
Dependant is immobile	0.51*	Carer feels physically tired	0.40*
With housework	0.38	Caring strains family relationships	0.38*
Carer feels physically tired	0.31*		
		6:*Restrictions on social life*	
2:*Carer/dependant relationship*		Caring affects social life	0.69*
Dependant is unappreciative	0.75	Carer has no time for friends	0.67*
Dependant doesn't help carer	0.72*	Carer has no private time	0.64*
No meaningful relationship	0.61*	Carer has few holidays	0.62*
Dependant is manipulative	0.60*	Carer feels physically tired	0.43*
Dependant is too demanding	0.59*	Caring threatens emotional health	0.32*
No satisfaction from caring	0.56*		
Dependant's behaviour difficult	0.54	7:*Financial consequences*	
Dependant becomes agitated	0.45	Carer experiences financial problems	0.73*
Carer feels angry	0.44*	Caring lowers standard of living	0.70*
Dependant's behaviour upsetting	0.41	Caring threatens physical health	0.42*
		Caring affects sleep	0.37*
3:*Incontinence*			
Urinary incontinence at night	0.83	8:*Lack of family support*	
Urinary incontinence during day	0.83	Family don't help much	0.83*
Dependant is incontinent	0.78*	Relatives don't visit often	0.81*
Faecal incontinence at night	0.75	Carer feels angry	0.34*
Faecal incontinence during day	0.74		
Help required to toilet	0.33	9:*Lack of professional support*	
		Professionals don't help much	0.79*
4:*Dependant's confused behaviour*		Professionals don't understand carer's problems	0.78*
Difficulty with normal conversation	0.78		
Dependant is disorientated	0.77	10:*Family relationships*	
Dependant's behaviour upsetting	0.68	Carer has no time for family	0.77*
Dependant wanders	0.67	Caring threatens family relationships	0.53*
Dependant becomes agitated /aggressive	69	Dependant is manipulative	0.33*
Dependant's behaviour a problem	0.44*		
Dependant is immobile	-0.31	11:*Other problems*	
		Other problems	0.87**
		Needs help with housework	0.39

*These variables are taken from column A of the CPPC and indicate that the carer is exposed to these problems in his/her caring environment.

** A dichotomous variable indicating that the carer identified further problems to caring in the open questions.

NB Minus sign indicates the more mobile the greater the problem.

Seven factors emerged from the second analysis and these are given in Table 2. These factors came from the 30 items on the CPPC and indicate that a carer perceives a stimulus to which they are exposed as stressful. It is apparent that these factors fittingly subdivide the construct system of perceived stress into similar partitions to those derived from the totally independent analysis of the caring environment.

Factor analysis on the malaise inventory was carried out using SPSSX and a confirmatory factor analysis using LISREL VI (Joreskog & Sorbom 1985). Both analyses failed to identify a single common factor. This is contrary to recent work (Bebbington & Quine 1987) but reflects earlier evidence which questioned the unidimensional nature of the malaise inventory (Hirst 1983). Based on the original description of the malaise inventory as an instrument containing both physical and psychological symptoms (Rutter et al. 1970), and with supporting evidence from the present study (Grant et al. 1989), a two-factor solution for the malaise inventory was introduced (Table 3). These two factors are highly interpretable and neatly divide the construct of malaise into what we have termed physical and psychological components. It was this two-factor solution that was used as the dependent variable in the causal path analysis.

Causal path analysis

Factor scores on these two sets of factors (Tables 1 and 2) were then used as explanatory variables of the two malaise sub-scales (Table 3) in a causal path analysis using LISREL VI. The LISREL model (Joreskog & Sorbom 1984; Saris & Stronkhorst 1984) allows estimation and testing of causal models using maximum likelihood estimation of covariance structure. Linear structural equation models represent causal theories with proportional and additive effects. The variables which the model should account for are called endogenous variables. The predetermined variables which are not explained by other variables in the theory are called exogenous. The effect of the ith endogenous variable from the jth endogenous variable is donoted by $ß_{ij}$. The effect of the ith endogenous variable from the jth exogenous variable is denoted by γ_{ij}. If the data are standardized then $ß$ and γ represent path weights such that an increase in one standard deviation in the prior variable would cause an increase of $ß(\gamma)$ standard deviations in the endogenous variable.

Table 2
Stress factors

Factor	Factor loading	Factor	Factor loading
1:Carer/dependant relationship variable		**3:Physical demands of caring**	
Dependant is unappreciative	0.68	Help required with personal care	0.62
Dependant's behaviour a problem	0.64	Carer feels physically impaired	0.49
Dependant doesn't help carer	0.60	Dependant is immobile	0.46
Dependant is too demanding	0.58	Dependant is incontinent	0.46
Dependant is manipulative	0.57	Caring threatens physical health	0.45
No meaningful relationship	0.56	Caring affects sleep	0.41
No satisfaction from caring	0.47	Carer can't relax	0.35
Carer feels angry	0.37		
Caring threatens family relationships	0.35	**4:Restrictions on social life**	
Caring threatens emotional health	0.34	Carer has no time for friends	0.63
Carer feels guilty	0.32	Caring affects social life	0.62
Carer has no time for friends	0.32	Carer has few holidays	0.45
		Carer has no private time	0.36
2:Carer's reaction to caring		Caring threatens emotional health	0.35
Carer feels out of control	0.61		
Carer can't relax	0.56	**5:Lack of family support**	
Carer feels guilty	0.49	Family don't help much	0.80
Caring threatens emotional health	0.46	Relatives don't visit often	0.66
Carer has no private time	0.45		
Carer feels angry	0.39	**6:Lack of professional support**	0.95
Caring threatens family relationships	0.37	Professionals don't understand problems	
Caring threatens physical health	0.36	Professionals don't help much	0.54
Caring affects sleep	0.33		
		7:Financial consequences	
		Carer experiences financial problems	0.73
		Caring lowers standard of living	0.61

All variables are taken from column B of the CPPC and indicate that the carer was exposed to, and found stressful, certain aspects of caring.

Once a model has been formulated, the causal paths within the theory are specified, information about the covariances is obtained from the data, and LISREL estimates the causal effects and other parameters and tests the model against the data.

The type of model which was specified rests on few prior assumptions. It has few restrictions in that any prior abilities may affect any later ones. The aspects of the caring environment were taken as the exogenous variables, since those studies reviewed show carers to score highly on stress and malaise measures, and there can be little or no opportunity for stressed individuals to self-select as carers. These environment factors have then been allowed to affect all of the endogenous variables. (Both stresses specific to caring and general malaise factors. Thus gamma paths were allowed to run to all of the endogenous variables).

Furthermore, beta paths were allowed to run from the caring specific stressors to malaise factors. This type of fully saturated model initially fitted is shown in Figure 1.

The F factors, along with INT, a measure on a seven-point scale of the frequency of caring provision, are the exogenous variables. All possible causal paths (g) between these and all the stress (S) and malaise (M) factors were allowed, as were all possible paths (ß) from the stress variables to the malaise factors. Covariation between the complete set of variables within each column was also permitted.

Model specification

The model specification entails that the beta and gamma weights on the causal paths reflect specific direct causal weights between the variables controlling for all indirect effects, spurious relationships and joint effects. On completion, the saturated model was 'tuned' in progressive stages guided by the t-values of the paths in the model and the modification indices of those omitted (LISREL computes modification indices for all paths which are not specified in the theoretical model being tested. Paths with high-modification indices are those which would

Table 3
Factor structure: malaise inventory

Factor	Factor loading
1:*Psychological malaise variable*	
Does every little thing get on your nerves and wear you out	0.69
Are you easily upset and irritated	0.65
Are you constantly keyed up and jittery	0.62
Do you often feel miserable and depressed	0.62
Do you often get worried about things	0.54
Do people often annoy and irritate you	0.52
Do you have difficulty falling or staying asleep	0.49
Do you become scared for no good reason	0.49
Do you often get in a violent rage	0.48
Do you feel tired most of the time	0.46
Do you wake up unnecessarily early	0.40
Are you scared to be alone	0.38
Do you worry about your health	0.35
Is your appetite poor	0.34
Are you scared of going out or meeting people	0.33
2:*Physical malaise*	
Do you often suffer from an upset stomach	0.63
Do you suffer from indigestion	0.63
Do you have a twitching of head, shoulders or neck	0.50
Do you have bad pains in your eyes	0.44
Does your heart often race like mad	0.44
Do you often have bad headaches	0.44
Do you often have backache	0.41
Are you troubled with rheumatism or fibrositis	0.38
Do you worry about your health	0.37

NB For the sake of parsimony the wording of items in the above table does not correspond exactly to that in the malaise inventory as used in the present study. One variable, 'Have you ever had a nervous breakdown', did not load on to either of the two factors.

improve the fit of the model to the data if they were indeed specified in the original model). The final model had a goodness of fit index of 0.981 and does not deviate significantly from the data on the chi-squared goodness of fit test. It should be emphasized that LISREL has been used in an exploratory fashion due to the numerous possible models that could be reasonably postulated for such a diverse data set. However the resultant model is both theoretically plausible and empirically relevant. It explains 47% of the variance in 'psychological malaise' (M1) and 20% of the variance in 'physical malaise' (M2).

For the sake of clarity and simplicity the resultant models are presented here in diagrammatic form. In these diagrams, significant paths are indicated by arrows, the widths of which are linearly related to the size of their effects. The model for 'psychological malaise' is given in Figure 2 and that for 'physical malaise' in Figure 3.

Inspection of the model for psychological malaise reveals a number of striking features. Firstly it is a powerful model accounting for 47% of the variance. However it is apparent that certain factors have no explanatory power and these include the degree of physical care and assistance the dependant requires, levels of incontinence, the extent of the dependant's confused behaviour and the restrictions on the carer's social life. Furthermore, with the exception of factor 5, none of the environment factors exert any direct effect on malaise, but are all mediated via the perceived degree of stress that they are seen to cause. This is precisely what a transactional model of stress would predict.

From a close examination of the model it is clear that psychological malaise results from a complex interaction of factors. However, of those factors implicated four have a dominant role: the nature of

carer/dependant relationships; the carer's response to the caring role; a lack of family support; and adverse financial consequences. Of these four factors it is the nature of the carer's response to their role that is most important. The factor loadings (S2, Table 2) give an indication of which variables are dominant. It appears that malaise is most likely to occur when the carer feels out of control, unable to relax because of worry about caring and experiences guilt about the situation. In circumstances such as these the carer perceives their emotional well-being to be threatened. Malaise is heightened when the carer feels that the dependant does not appreciate their efforts and exhibits problem behaviour in terms of failing to help and being overly demanding and manipulative. Under these conditions carers find it difficult to sustain a meaningful relationship and consequently gain little satisfaction (S1, Figure 2).

Those factors relating to lack of family support and the financial consequences of caring are largely self-explanatory, but are given support by the empirical literature which suggests that it is most often one family member who shoulders the main burden of care (Wicks & Henwood 1988).

In a multivariate analysis of this type, a case can always be argued that the results represent an artefact of the measurement process as much as they do the empirical reality. Fortunately, in the present study, powerful supporting evidence for the multivariate results is provided by a content analysis of 657 open-ended statements on the problems of caring and 546 such statements on the satisfactions of caring. The categories created during this phase of the analysis mirror almost exactly those produced from the factor analysis, yet the qualitative work was completed 3 months prior to the statistical analyses reported here.

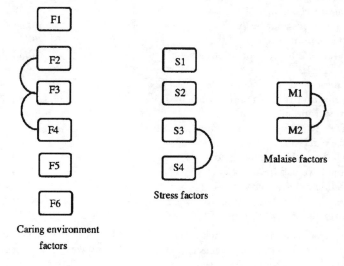

Figure 1

Environment factors   Stress factors   Malaise factors

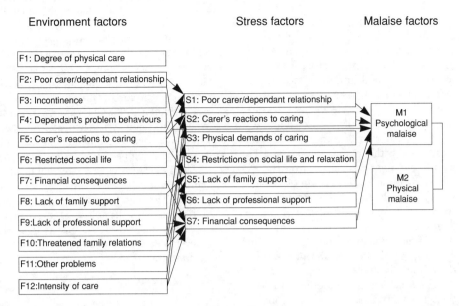

Figure 2

Model for physical malaise

Figure 3 shows the model for physical malaise and it will be seen that it is less powerful than that for psychological malaise, explaining only 20% of the variance. Furthermore, in contrast to the model for psychological malaise, the explanatory variables, whilst being largely similar, exert their influence directly and not via their perceived stressfulness. It should also be noted that the dominant explanatory factor is the same as for psychological malaise but that the presence of variables relating to physical health, albeit at lower factor loadings, needs to be borne in mind. The occurrence of a high modification factor (36.7) back from physical malaise to the perceived stress caused by the physical demands of caring is

of particular interest. This suggests that the physical demands of caring are not perceived as stressful until carers are themselves experiencing physical symptoms, indicating that whilst they are in good physical health carers do not find the physical demands of caring overly burdensome. The absence of any direct relationship between the physical demands of caring and physical malaise, but the direct influence of feelings of being out of control, guilt and so on (F5), highlights the central role of such reactions in furthering our understanding of both psychological and physical malaise. These results, together with those previously described from the qualitative analysis (Nolan & Grant 1989), have implications for practice issues relating to informal carers and it is to this area that attention is now turned.

Environment factors   Stress factors   Malaise factors

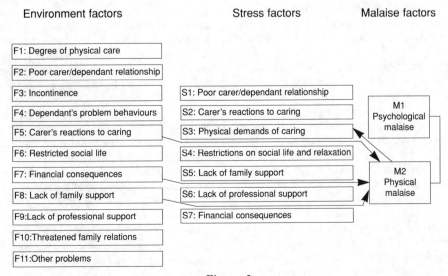

Figure 3

Discussion

In the introduction to this paper it was argued that, despite the burgeoning of research in the field of informal care, it is still not clear which aspects of caring are the most stressful and how such stress might best be alleviated. Consideration of previous attempts to operationalise and measure carer burden identifies similar deficits and it was suggested that carer burden might be better understood within a transactional model of stress. The empirical evidence from the present study using a triangulation of methods and data would appear to substantiate this suggestion. Taken together these results highlight the importance of the carer's perceptions of the demands of the caring role, the extent to which they feel out of control of their situation and experience feelings of guilt and the central position of their relationship with their dependant. Carer malaise is also more likely when there is a lack of family support and adverse financial burdens imposed by caring and when the carer perceives these as stressful. These results can help to inform important practice decisions relating to the provision of services for carers and their dependants, which reinforce and extend those arguments previously posited (Nolan & Grant 1989). There it was suggested that service providers, and more particularly nurses, adopt an educative/supportive model in their interactions with carers and their dependants. Such an approach is underpinned by the acceptance of a transactional model of stress and the present analyses add to the validity of such assumptions.

Furthermore it seems clear that appropriate service provision needs to be informed by a detailed knowledge of carer/dependant relationships. Such knowledge is unlikely to be gained from a cursory assessment but requires a degree of trust between carer, dependant and the service provider. Such trust is best established where there is a sharing of caring tasks and regular contact between all parties. Given the high dependency and levels of disability with which many carers are faced, this places nurses in the unique position of providing care of an often very personal nature to the dependant, whilst also having the professional knowledge and expertise to give the carer advice, support and training.

This however requires a delicate balance in acquiring the trust of carer and dependant whilst giving due cognisance to both their needs (Hasselkus 1988, Thorne & Robinson 1988). A failure to achieve this balance can result in dependants feeling discredited (Charmaz 1983) and losing trust in the professionals' judgement (Thorne & Robinson 1988), with carers perceiving the quality of care as poor. Such considerations apply in both community (Hasselkus 1988) and institutional settings (Bowers 1988).

Whilst the notion of nurses making wider use of a stress/adaptation approach to their care is not new (Craig & Edwards 1983, Clarke 1984a,b), it is encouraging to see it resurfacing in conjunction with a nursing model (Watkins 1988). However, in order to make optimal use of such approaches in providing a service to carers and their dependants, there is a need to incorporate wider research evidence which extends our conceptualisation of what constitutes caring (Bowers 1987) and provides a relevant theoretical basis for the enhanced understanding of carer/dependant relationships (Quershi 1986, Quershi & Walker 1986, Phillips & Rempusheski 1986).

Service providers

Balancing the requirements of carer and dependant with a relevant role for service providers has been further informed by the use of a family systems approach (Boss 1988, Chilman et al. 1988). A most useful synthesis of such a paradigm within a typology of chronic illness and disability has been provided by Rolland (1988). This can act as a central reference point in taking the debate beyond the level of the medical model, whose utility is increasingly questioned (Allan & Hall 1988) and yet within which many practitioners remain trapped (Oliver 1988).

At the end of the day, if nursing is to offer an individual approach to the service we provide to dependency groups and their carers, then the issues raised above will need to be addressed. It is hoped that this paper will provide further stimulus for nurses and other professional groups to extend their knowledge and expertise in this increasingly important area.

References

Allan J.D. & Hall B.A. (1988) Challenging the focus of technology – a critique of the medical model in a changing health care system. *Advances in Nursing Science* **10**(3), 22-34.

Bebbington A. & Quine L. (1987) A comment on Hirst's 'Evaluating the Malaise Inventory'. *Social Psychiatry* **22**, 5-7.

Bell R., Gibbons R. & Pinchen I. (1987) *Action Research with Informal Carers: Patterns and Processes in Carers' Lives. Report on Phase 2.* Health Promotion Service, Cambridge.

Bonny S. (1984) *Who Cares in Southward.* Association of Carers, Rochester, Kent.

Boss P. (1988) *Family Stress Management.* Sage, California.

Bowers B.J. (1987) Intergenerational caregiving: adult caregivers and their ageing parents. *Advances in Nursing Science* **9**(2), 20-31.

Bowers B.J. (1988) Family perceptions of care in a nursing home. *The Gerontologist* 28(3), 361-366.

Bowling A. (1984) Caring for the elderly widowed – the burden on their supporters. *British Journal of Social Work* 14, 435-455.

Briggs A. (1983) *Who Cares?* Association of Carers, Rochester, Kent.

Brody E.M. (1985) Parent care as a normative family stress. *The Gerontologist* 21, 19-29.

Cantor M.H. (1983) Strain among caregivers: A Study of experience in the United States. *The Gerontologist* 26(6), 597-604.

Challis D. (1985) *Case Management and Consumer Choice – The Community Care Scheme*. Personal Social Services Unit, discussion paper 396. University of Kent, Canterbury.

Charmaz K. (1983) Loss of self – A fundamental form of suffering in the chronically ill. *Sociology of Health and Illness* 5(2), 168-195.

Chilman C.S., Nunnally E.W. & Cox F.M. (1988) *Chronic Illness and Disability. Families in Trouble Series*, Vol.2. Sage, California.

Clarke, M. (1984a) Stress and coping: constructs for nursing. *Journal of Advanced Nursing* 9, 3-13.

Clarke M. (1984b) The constructs of stress and coping as a rationale for nursing activities. *Journal of Advanced Nursing* 9, 267-275.

Craig H.M. & Edwards J.E. (1983) Adaptation in chronic illness: an eclectic model for nurses. *Journal of Advanced Nursing* 5, 475-484.

Eagles J.M., Craig A., Rawlinson F., Restall D.B., Beattie J.A.G. & Besson J.A.O. (1987) The psychological well-being of supporters of the demented elderly. *British Journal of Psychiatry* 150, 293-298.

Equal Opportunities Commission (1982a) *Caring for the Elderly and Handicapped: Community Care Policies and Womens' Lives*. EOC, Manchester.

Equal Opportunities Commission (1982b) *Who Cares for the Carers? Opportunities for those Caring for the Elderly and Handicapped*. EOC, Manchester.

Fengler A.P. & Goodrich N. (1979) Wives of disabled men: the hidden patients. *The Gerontologist* 19(2), 175-183.

Fitting M., Rabin P., Lucas M.J. & Eastham J. (1986) Caregivers for dementia patients: a comparison of husbands and wives. *The Gerontologist* 26(3), 248-252.

George L.K. & Gwyther L.P. (1986) Caregiver well-being: a multidimensional examination of family caregivers of demented adults. *The Gerontologist* 26(3), 253-259.

Gilleard C.J., Belford M., Gilleard E., Whittick J.E. & Gledhill K. (1984) Emotional distress amongst caregivers of the elderly mentally infirm. *British Journal of Psychiatry* 145, 172-177.

Goosen G.M. & Bush H.A. (1979) Adaptation – a feedback process. *Advances in Nursing Science* 1(4), 91-100.

Grant G., Nolan M.R. & Ellis N. (1989) *A Reappraisal of the Malaise Inventory*. CSPRD working paper, University College of North Wales, Bangor.

Green H. (1988) *Informal Carers. General Household Survey 1985*. Series GHS No.15, Supplement 16. Social Survey Division, OPCS. HMSO, London.

Gwyther L.P. & George L.K. (1986) Caregivers for dementia patients: complex determinants of well-being and burden. *The Gerontologist* 26(3), 245-247.

Hasselkus B.R. (1988) Meaning in family caregiving: Perspectives on caregiver/professional relationship. *The Gerontologist* 25(5), 686-691.

Hatfield A.B. (1987) Coping and adaptation: a conceptual framework for understanding families. In *Families of the Mentally Ill: Coping and Adaptation*. (Hatfield A.B. & Lefley H.P. eds), Cassell Educational, London.

Hawranik P. (1985) Caring for aging parents: divided allegiances. *Journal of Geriatric Nursing* 11(10), 19-22.

Henwood M. & Wicks M. (1984) *The Forgotten Army: Family Care and Elderly People*. Briefing Paper. Family Policies Study Centre, London.

Hirschfield M.J. (1981) Families living and coping with the cognitively impaired. In *Care of the Ageing* (Copp L.A. ed.), Churchill Livingstone, Edinburgh.

Hirschfield M.J. (1983) Homecare versus institutionalisation: family caregivers and senile brain disease. *International Journal of Nursing Studies* 20(1), 23-32.

Hirschfield M.J. & Krulick T. (1985) Family caregiving to severely chronically ill children and the aged. In *Longterm Care of the Elderly. Recent Advances in Nursing* 15 (King K. ed.), Churchill Livingstone, Edinburgh.

Hirst M. (1983) Evaluating the malaise inventory: an item analysis. *Social Psychiatry* 18, 181-184.

Hooyman N., Gonyea J. & Montgomery R. (1985) The impact of in-home services termination on family caregivers. *The Gerontologist* 4(2), 141-145.

Jacobson S.F. (1983) An overview of coping. In *Nurses under Stress* (Jacobson S.F. & McGrath H.M. eds.), Wiley, New York.

Joreskog K.G. & Sorbom D. (1984) LISREL VI *User's Guide*. University of Uppsala, Uppsala.

Joreskog K.G. & Sorbom D. (1985) LISREL VI: *Analysis of Linear Structural Relationships by Maximum Likelihood, Instrumental and Least Squares Method*. University of Uppsala. Uppsala.

Kosberg J.I & Cairl R.E. (1986) The cost of care index: as case management tool for screening informal carers. *The Gerontologist* 26(3), 273-278.

Motenko A.K. (1989) The frustrations, gratifications and well-being of dementia caregivers. *The Gerontologist* 29(2), 166-172.

Nolan M.R. & Grant G. (1989) Addressing the needs of informal carers: a neglected area of nursing practice. *Journal of Advanced Nursing* 14(11), 950-961.

Oliver M. (1988) Flexible services. *Nursing Times* 84(14), 25-29.

Parker G. (1985) *With Due Care and Attention: A Review of Research on Informal Care.* Occasional paper No.2. Family Policy Studies Centre, London.

Phillips L.R. & Rempusheski V.F. (1986) Caring for the frail elderly at home: toward a theoretical explanation of the dynamics of poor quality family caregiving. *Advances in Nursing Science* 8(4), 62-84.

Phillipson C. (1988) *Planning for Community Care: Facts and Fallacies in the Griffiths Report. Working paper* 1. Centre for Social Gerontology, Keele University.

Poulshock W.S. & Deimling G.T (1984) Families caring for elders in residence: Issues in the measurement of burden. *Journal of Gerontology* 39(2), 230-239.

Quine L. & Charnley H. (1987) The malaise inventory as a measure of stress in carers. In *Evaluating Support to Informal Carers* (Twigg J. ed.), Conference papers. York University, York.

Qureshi H. (1986) Responses to dependency: reciprocity, affect and power in family relationships. *In Dependency and Interdependency in Old Age: Theoretical Perspectives and Policy Alternatives* (Phillipson C., Bernard M. & Strang R. eds.), Croom Helm, London.

Qureshi H. & Walker A. (1986) Caring for elderly people: the family and the state. In *Ageing and Social Policy: a Critical Assessment* (Phillipson C. & Walker A. eds.), Gower, Aldershot.

Robinson B.C. (1983) Validation of a caregiver strain index. *Journal of Gerontology* 38(3), 344-348.

Rolland J.S. (1988) A conceptual model of chronic and life threatening illness and its impact on families. In *Illness and Disability. Families in Trouble Series.* Vol.2 (Chilman C.S., Nunnally E.W. & Cox F.M. eds.), Sage, Beverly Hills.

Rutter M., Graham P. & Yule W. (1970) *A Neuropsychiatric Study in Childhood.* Heinemann, London.

Sandford J. (1975) Tolerance of debility in elderly dependants by supporters at home. *British Medical Journal* 3, 471-473.

Saris W.E. & Stronkhorst H.L. (1984) *Causal Modelling in Nonexperimental Research.* Sociometric Research Foundation, Amsterdam.

Scott D.W., Oberst M.T. & Cropkin M.J. (1980) A stress-coping model. *Advances in Nursing Science* 3(1), 9-23.

Silverstein N.M. (1984) Informing the elderly about public services: The relationship between sources of knowledge and service utilisation. *The Gerontologist* 24(1), 37-40.

Spaniol L. & Jung H. (1987) Effective coping: a conceptual model. In *Families of the Mentally Ill*: Coping and Adaptation (Hatfield A.B. & Lefley H.P. eds.), Cassell, London.

Thompson D.M. (1987) *Calling All Carers.* Association of Carers, South Manchester Branch.

Thorne S.E. & Robinson C.A. (1988) Reciprocal trust in healthcare relationships. *Journal of Advanced Nursing* 13, 782-789.

Tomlin S. (1989) *Abuse of Elderly People: An Unnecessary and Preventable Problem.* British Geriatrics Society, London.

Twigg J. (1986) Introduction: *Evaluating Support to Informal Carers.* Conference papers, University of York, York.

Watkins M. (1988) Lifting the burden. *Geriatric Nursing and Home Care* 8(9), 18-20.

Wicks M. & Henwood M. (1988) The demographic and social circumstances of elderly people. In *Mental Health Problems in Old Age* (Gearing B., Johnson M. & Heller T. eds.), Wiley, Chichester.

Winogrond I.R., Fisk A.A., Kirsling R.A. & Keynes B. (1987) The relationship between caregiver burden and morale to Alzheimer's disease patients functioning in a therapeutic setting. *The Gerontologist* 27(3), 336-339.

Worcester M.I. & Quayhagen M.P. (1983) Correlates of caregiving satisfaction: prerequisites to elder home care. *Research in Nursing and Health* 6, 61-67.

Wright F.D. (1986) *Left to Care Alone.* Gower, Aldershot.

Zarit S.H., Reever K.E. & Bach-Peterson J. (1980) Relatives of the impaired elderly: correlates of feeling of burden. *The Gerontologist* 29(6), 649-655.

Zarit S.H. & Zarit J.M. (1982) *Measuring Burden and Support in Families with Alzheimer's Disease Elders.* Paper presented at the 35th Annual Scientific Meeting of the Gerontological Society of America, Boston, Massachusetts.

Zarit S.H., Todd P.A. & Zarit J.M. (1986) Subjective burden of husbands and wives as caregivers: a longitudinal study. *The Gerontologist* 26(3), 260-266.

Models of carers: How do social care agencies conceptualise their relationship with informal carers?

RESOURCE 2

Julia Twigg
Journal of Social Policy
18, pp 53-66, 1989.
Published by Cambridge
University Press

Abstract

Carers occupy an ambiguous position within the social care system. Services are predominantly structured around the dependant rather than the carer, and this has important consequences for their delivery and evaluation. Many of the problems that arise in thinking about carer issues relate to confusion over the way the relationship between social care agencies and informal carers should be perceived. The paper outlines three models that provide frames of reference for this relationship: carers as resources; carers as co-workers; and carers as co-clients. The tensions between these are then used to explore the contradictions of policy in this field.

Introduction

Informal carers pose certain problems to social care agencies that are not simply those of resources or of care management, but that have their roots in difficulties that are more conceptual in character. How should one envisage the relationships between agencies and the informal sector? What obligations do agencies have towards carers? How indeed should one term such individuals or groups: as carers, as the informal sector, as informal networks, or simply as the family? Each of these terms has different connotations and will as a result produce a different structuring of the issues.

These essentially conceptual difficulties underlie much of the confusion of purpose and activity in this area. The relationship between carers and social care agencies is an uncertain, ill defined one, and this in turn underwrites the limited, even primitive, character of much of the evaluative work in this field (Twigg, 1988). In this paper I shall explore the roots of these difficulties in the ambiguous position of carers within the social care system, suggesting that agencies have available to them three major models or ideal types of their relationship with carers. Having developed, rather schematically, the logical element within these ideal types, I shall go on to use the tensions between them to explore some of the contradictions of policy.

The ambiguous position of carers

There are two ways in which the ambiguous position of carers within the social care system can be expressed. First, carers are on the margins of the social care system. They are in some senses within its remit, part of the subject of its concern and responsibility, and yet are at the same time beyond its remit, part of the taken-for-granted background to provision, the 'out-there' against which agencies act.

The second way in which the ambiguous position of carers can be expressed is in terms of their 'off-centre' character. They – or rather their outcomes – are in a sense only 'by-products' of the care system. They are not its main focus. To this degree therefore they exist 'off-centre' to it. Often, indeed, they are the means to an end, and their well-being, or concern for the dependant, or level of activity, form only the intermediate outcomes of the system which is essentially focused elsewhere. Inevitably, then, concern with carer welfare has something of an instrumental quality to it.

Because of these fundamental ambiguities, social care agencies such as social service departments have no single, straightforward model of their relationship with carers. Rather they operate within the context of a series of different models, or rather, frames of reference. Each of these different frames of reference conceptualises the subject differently, and each has different implications for policy and for intervention. Agencies operate in the context of a series of such frames of reference, cutting from one to another according to the demands of the particular situation.

The emphases that will be placed on the different frames of reference will vary according to the organisational context. Here I will largely be concerned with the implications of such models for social service departments. However, much of what I say applies also to health care agencies, to voluntary bodies and to other social care agencies within the social policy world that interact with carers, although each of these will have their own particular emphases. There will also inevitably be variation between different local authorities. A department in one area may, as part of a policy initiative, put greater emphasis on the subjective well-being of carers, as opposed to the requirement to reduce the levels of institutionalisation that may be in the forefront of policy in another area. Despite such policy differences, however, all departments, I would suggest, relate in some degree to the frames of reference for carers that I shall outline. These frames of reference are common to the culture of the social services.

Lastly, there will be important variation in the emphases between the differing levels of the organisation. Thus the pressures upon and conceptual needs of senior managers will be different from those of front-line practitioners. It is likely, for example, that managers will be more alive to resource aspects while front-line practitioners are more concerned with carer well-being. The political pressures upon publicly accountable authority members will produce different emphases yet again.

Three models of carers

Turning now to the substance of the relationship of departments to carers, I want to suggest that these cross-cutting frames of reference can, for ease of discussion, be condensed into three principal ones. These are: *carers as resources, carers as co-workers and carers as co-clients*. These represent three ideal types of orientation of agencies towards carers. As such they are intentionally schematic. I should emphasise at this point that I am not attempting to describe in any adequate way the full complexities of practice or the full range of responses found within departments. Social service departments and other agencies operate within highly political environments: political both in the sense of the internal politics of the organisation and the external politics of welfare provision. As a result models of carers and of the agency's relationship to them are multiple and enmeshed in the even greater complexity of the agency's aims and activities. In suggesting these three models, therefore, I am not attempting to provide what Geertz would describe as Thick Description (Geertz, 1973), but rather, a schematic account based on three ideal types of the relationship of the agencies to informal care. Tracing the logical implications of these ideal types will, I hope, allow us to explore some of the inherent contradictions of social policy in this field.

Carers as resources

The first model is that of *carers as resources*. Recent work on informal care has reinforced our understanding of how it is the informal sector that is predominantly involved in the support of elderly people. Simple ideas about advanced industrial countries failing to support their elderly have been replaced by a better understanding of the degree to which the old kinship patterns of obligation still operate. Anxieties have been expressed about the consequences of demographic trends, particularly in relation to the dependency ratio; further anxieties have also been expressed concerning social and cultural changes, particularly in relation to the consequences of divorce and of higher rates of female participation in the labour market (Moroney, 1976; 1986; Wicks, 1982; Rimmer and Wicks, 1983). But the majority of analysts would follow Finch (Finch, 1987) in her estimation of the likely continuance of such patterns of responsibility and caregiving, though, of course, Finch views such a continuance as a far from satisfactory one.

The reality therefore remains that the vast majority of care to frail and dependent people is provided by the informal sector. It represents the 'given', the taken-for-granted reality against which services are structured. This simple fact alone requires that departments and other agencies recognise carers as a major form of resource. But they are a form of resource unlike any other, in two particular ways.

First, formal and informal are here not of equal normative status. Informal is prior to formal. Thus, though there may in theory be substitution between the two forms of provision, on the model of the substitution of different resources in the productive process, such substitution is in fact quite narrowly constrained by normative assumptions that give preference to provision by the informal sector. This is true both within the perceptions of agencies and in the wider social world. It is not the case, for example, when we talk about the mixed economy of welfare that the different forms of provision are of equal status, and there is not, therefore, true substitution between the two forms of care. Informal is in this sense prior. Social care agencies like social services thus operate, with regard to carers, an essentially residualist model in which the agency responds to the deficiencies of the care network.

This residualism is itself constrained, as we shall see when we turn to the two other ideal types, by some of the cross-cutting demands implicit in those other, parallel, models. I am not arguing therefore that agencies are exclusively residualist in their approach. Residualism is, however, a central aspect of agencies' perceptions of carers, and it underpins the ways in which, in this model of carers as resources, the informal sector represents 'the given', the – as it were – 'out there' backdrop to formal provision that exists prior to and quite separate from those formal services.

The second sense in which *carers as resources* are unlike any other form of resource is that they are not subject to the formal laws of supply and demand. They are an essentially uncommandable resource that cannot be created by policy decision, nor can they be turned on or off by patterns of incentives and disincentives. As has become increasingly clear from recent work on the informal sector, it is long-term social factors, notably kinship, that create the potentiality for informal caregiving. Social and cultural factors, in relation to, for example, employment or women's expectations, in turn impinge on these, determining the actual pattern and levels of such availability (Abrams, 1977; Abrams and Bulmer, 1985; Bulmer, 1987). These factors, however, operate at the level of society in general. As a result the pattern of the availability of informal carers remains in any extensive sense beyond the influence of agencies. This is despite the rather unrealistic hopes of the Barclay Report and the rosier accounts of some of the exponents of community action (Allen, 1983).

Carers are an uncommandable resource in a second, more micro, way also. Whatever moral influence agencies or the wider policy world may attempt to exert on kin or other potential carers, the decision whether or not to take up caregiving responsibility remains with the individual. It is, furthermore, largely taken off-stage, beyond the influence of formal agencies, though not beyond the influence of other kin. Carer involvement is thus not something which any agency can control or even influence to a marked extent. This is even more the case in regard to the sorts of tasks that particular carers are willing to undertake, to the way in which these tasks are performed, and to the emotional tone which accompanies them. Carers are not subject to supervision or control and they are, therefore, an *undirectable* as well as an *uncommandable* resource.

It is in this sense also, as well as in the residualism that we noted earlier, that agencies in conceiving of carers as resources are responding to what is a primary and prior reality, rather than attempting to influence or determine that reality. Our picture of carers as resources is one that thus contains certain constraints.

We turn now to the implications for policy and practice of this model. The central aim of agencies in such a resource frame of reference is care maximisation: the maintenance and perhaps marginal increase of levels of informal support. The central task of such an approach therefore is to understand the nature of the informal sector, to appreciate its character and to understand its structure, both in its potentialities and its limitations. Who does what? What sorts of

relationships will bear what sorts of tasks? What are the differences between what friends and neighbours will do to give support, and what only close kin will do? What are the demographic constraints posed in different areas? All these are issues that fall within the context of a resource framework, and all bear on the potentialities of the informal sector.

The resource model places its central focus on the dependant. The informal carers form only a background to these – a vital resource background, of course – but one that is not the primary subject of the agency's concern. Thus although agencies may be concerned to understand the *character* of this objectively given background, they are not – in this model – concerned with the subjective interests of the carers who make up this background. Concern with carer welfare in this model is therefore marginal, and will be overridden by concern lest services undermine or take over from what is seen as the prior family responsibility. Fears of the substitution of formal inputs for informal care will be predominant, and conflicts of interest between carer and dependant will effectively be ignored.

I should reiterate at this point that I am approaching the issue in a deliberately schematic way. The model I have outlined does not represent the approach taken by any particular agency. It is rather one of the frames of reference in terms of which agencies operate. These frames of reference, as I have already suggested, are held in plurality, and agencies will shift between them according to the pressures of the particular circumstances and the needs of policy in relation to them.

Carers as co-workers

The second ideal type or frame of reference is that of *carers as co-workers*. Here agencies work in parallel with the informal sector, aiming at a co-operative and enabling role.

The social construction of the term 'carer', and the rapid growth of its use within social service departments and other social care agencies is itself part of this process whereby kin and friendship relations are semi-professionalised and brought within the orbit of the formal system. Carers here become co-workers in the care enterprise.

This approach stands in contrast to the first frame of reference in which the informal sector was seen as providing an object-like and separate background to agency provision. Here, by contrast, the aim is to overcome the separation and to link the two sectors. The dominant image is that of Bayley's metaphor of the 'interweaving' of the two forms of provision (Bayley, 1973).

Essentially more attractive to the liberal instincts of social service and other front line practitioners than the earlier resource model, it is an approach that still raises considerable difficulties. The roots of these lie in the essentially different normative bases that underpin the formal and informal sectors. The formal sector is governed by the classic features of rational-legal authority: it is universalistic in approach, affectively neutral, and governed by rules of procedure and accountability by which situations are assessed separately from the status or personal characteristics of individuals. It rests on a formal knowledge base, in which professionals are trained, and acquire particular technical skills. The informal sector by contrast is particularistic, marked by strong affect, frequently characterised by long-term reciprocity or by effectively inalienable relationships, and by ascriptive status judgements. Its knowledge base is rooted in daily experience and assumed to be open to all. It is a knowledge of persons and of localities.

It is because of these essential differences that the two systems do not mesh easily or happily together. Abrams, and others, have explored some of the difficulties in this field (Bulmer and Abrams, 1986; Froland, 1981; Bayley, 1982).

Turning again to the implications for policy and practice, the aim of intervention in this co-worker model is a mixed one – certainly to maintain and enable informal care, but in ways that recognise the importance, particularly the instrumental importance, of carer morale.

Good carer morale clearly contributes both to the likelihood that care will continue to be offered, and to the quality of the care that is offered. The co-worker model therefore encompasses the carer's interest and the carer's morale within its concerns, but based on what is essentially an instrumental motive. Maintaining high carer morale and involvement thus represents an intermediate outcome on the way to the final outcome of increased welfare for the dependent person.

In unsophisticated versions, conflicts of interest in this model are either ignored, with the assumption (based on some reality) that carers do predominantly want to care for their dependants, or are seen as something that can be collapsed into individual negotiations – perhaps social worker enabled – at the micro level.

Carers as co-clients

Thirdly, there is the frame of reference that regards *carers as co-clients*. The definition of the client is itself a problematic one; and within social services at least 'the client' remains an essentially contestable concept. This is illustrated, more generally, in some of the debates concerning the status and treatment of elderly people in the care system. In the medical sphere 'patients' can be defined – at least in the formal model – as people with medical needs or people in the context of their medical needs. In the area of social care, however, the definitions are much more problematic. 'Social care' lacks the boundary keeping that elite medical knowledge and professional groupings provide. As a result, social work definitions remain disputed, open to social and political scrutiny, criticism and redefinition.

This general quality of social care definitions applies particularly strongly to questions of the conceptualisation of carers, and the appropriateness of the application of the term 'client' to carers. For here departments are beyond the normal, essentially substantive, definition of their remit, and involved in areas that merge imperceptibly into general social life and its responsibilities. To regard carers as co-clients, therefore, threatens, on the one side, an imperialistic take-over of what are normal processes of life; and on the other, a swamping of the social care system with 'ordinary misery'.

Parallels with child care work where the family may be taken as the focus of the welfare intervention, though more useful in the context of the carers of disabled or mentally handicapped children, from which much of the carer literature derives, are less helpful in the context of carers of adults where the normative assumptions concerning the relationships are essentially different. In child care cases, parents have rights over the child, rights to the child and responsibilities for the child, all of which are relatively well-defined and assumed. By contrast, in the case of disabled adults and elderly people, even where highly dependent, they retain the moral status of adults. Their relationship with their carers is by its nature more voluntaristic and open to negotiation. This voluntarism is both a fact of social life, and a moral principle that agencies recognise in their own dealings with the carers of adults. It also compromises the degree to which the family as a whole, in the case of adults, can be taken as the unit of intervention.

The major exception to this relates to spouse-carers, who form a distinctive subgroup of carers. Here the normative ties of obligation are more clearly defined and are stronger. In the case of elderly couples, the age and possible disability of the spouse carer means that they are often defined as a form of co-client. With younger, fitter spouses, the definitions are less clear, and the carer is more likely to be perceived as a resource or 'co-worker'.

The general criteria whereby carers do or do not become defined as clients are complex. In practice, the usage tends to be focused on the 'heavy end' of caregiving and on the most heavily stressed individuals.

Even here, however, their status as clients is never a fully equal one, and carers remain at best secondary clients rather than fully co-clients.

The aim of intervention in terms of this framework is the relief of carer strain; the concept of strain is sometimes here reinterpreted in terms of a medical model of stress. This operates as a means of legitimating the definition of the carer as client or patient and thus of policing the boundaries of normal life referred to earlier. This is the frame of reference, of course, in which conflicts of interest between carer and dependant are fully recognised.

The relationship of formal and informal

We have thus moved, rather schematically, between three frames of reference. In these frames of reference the relationship between the formal and informal shifts. In the first – the model of carers as resources – the informal sector provides the objective background to provision. It represents the *given* against which agencies act, and against which they structure their services. It is a frame of reference that has a neutral quality to it. Agencies relate to the informal sector as an object-like reality. They read the situation, and act in its context. Their primary concern is to understand the nature of the phenomenon, but they have essentially *no obligation* towards it.

In the second model – that of carers as co-workers – the informal sector has, as it were, moved over from its object-like and separate status into that where there is a slightly uneasy intermingling between the formal and informal sectors. Here the world of informal care is still something separate from that of formal provision, but it has become the object of social service support. Agencies here no longer simply aim to observe and understand a phenomenon, but relate more actively to it, enabling, encouraging and supporting areas, but in an essentially co-opting and instrumental way.

Lastly, in the third frame of reference – that of carers as co-clients – the informal sector has moved over into the ambit of agencies, and carers have become fully integrated into the concerns of agencies. With this they become the subject of obligation for the agency, which can no longer simply regard them as resources to be exploited or workers to be co-opted, but has to recognise a different and essentially obligatory relationship.

The definition of carers

I have in this paper deliberately used both the terms 'informal care' and 'carers', although they have, of course, different emphases and significance. This is because the definition of the subject is itself prone to shifting emphases

according to the particular frame of reference in operation. Thus a perception of carers as resources or as co-workers requires agencies to recognise the potentialities of the informal sector as widely as possible, attempting to work with and co-opt all potential sources of informal support. Here the definition of 'carer' is drawn very wide, and indeed is merged into concepts of the 'informal sector' or – more politically – 'the caring capacity of the community'.

By contrast, where the emphasis is on carers as co-clients, a quite different and much narrower definition is employed. Here the emphasis is no longer on fluidity or the interpenetration of formal and informal sectors, but upon boundary keeping and on the close definition of a limited set of heavily burdened carers.

The contradictions of policy

I want to turn briefly now to the ways in which these different models of the relationship between carers and agencies expose some of the contradictions within policy. I should emphasise here that in talking about contradictions, I am not implying any easy criticism of policymakers. The contradictions I shall refer to are inherent ones, implicit within the structure of the various relationships and the demands placed upon them, and there is no simple resolution to these tensions.

The first form of tension is that between *prevention* and *substitution*. Agencies often express a wish to act preventatively to support carers, providing services that will ease their lot and strengthen their involvement. But at the same time anxieties are expressed that such services will substitute for informal care and will encourage people to do less for their dependants. This latter fear has been strengthened by the recent criticisms of the New Right with their emphasis on family obligation and the need not to undermine this by incentive systems that 'encourage' people to substitute welfare provision for their own activities. Concrete evidence to support the existence of such patterns of trade-offs is, however, notably absent. Nonetheless, this tension between supporting and substituting relates in many ways to the distinction made earlier between regarding carers as co-workers, in some way co-operatively involved in the care enterprise, and regarding them as resources whose levels of activity must not be undermined.

It is certainly a familiar criticism expressed by many carers that if they appear to be managing, they get praise from practitioners, but no practical help to support the continuance of that managing. The system appears therefore to 'reward' failure rather than success. Services in this view come too late and are focused too narrowly on situations that are already near to collapse. This is an argument put forward by Fennell et al. (1981) in their evaluation of day care, where they question the appropriateness in certain cases of using the service to shore up situations, often at considerable cost to the carer, that are essentially on the edge of breakdown. Such action, they argue, merely prolongs an intolerable situation. Gilleard et al. (1984) make a similar point in relation to the intervention of a psychogeriatric day hospital.

This brings us to a slightly different aspect of the same problem of acting preventatively. The emphasis in service provision on those near to collapse is one of the consequences of taking passage into residential care as a crucial service indicator. The relatively high cost of residential care, its general unpopularity as a form of support and its clear and objective character as an event all contribute to making it a particularly widely used service indicator. But such potential residential care cases are by definition those on the borderline, close to collapse. A policy targeted on them is therefore open to the criticisms voiced above concerning the inappropriateness and almost, in the case of certain carers, the cruelty of focusing resources on shoring up such essentially unstable situations.

The consequences, by contrast, of focusing on 'successful' care situations is to place resources where they may not be the greatest immediate need. It can mean in effect abandoning certain very stressed situations as beyond 'real' relief and essentially unstable in their character. Where the situation concerns an elderly person alone, this harsh decision does occur and does indeed often result in institutionalisation. Social service departments and health care agencies do effectively determine the point at which they will not support a person in the community, though such support might theoretically be possible. Though it is a resource-based decision it tends to remain hidden behind practice considerations. Where informal carers are involved, however, the ramifications are in a sense less clear. A failure or refusal by agencies to support at these levels of pressure, because once again they are deemed to be situations unstable in their character and beyond 'real' relief, may indeed result in care breakdown, but it may more simply result in the redoubling of stress for the carer, for some period at least. There is a genuine tension, therefore, and one that has difficult ethical consequences in relation to carers, between focusing on preventative support or on marginal situations.

The second major form of contradiction concerns the tension between supporting carers so as to ensure the continuance of caregiving and supporting carers to increase their well-being. This is the major tension

that runs through policy in relation to carers, and it underlies the subsequent areas of contradiction that I shall refer to below.

It tends to be assumed in a general, rather liberal, way that supporting carers so as to ensure the continuance of caregiving and supporting carers to increase their well-being go together, whereas they are, in fact, analytically quite separate. They represent essentially the difference between a focus on carers as co-workers and carers as clients. In the latter models carers have outcomes per se and their morale is one of the final ends of the system. In the former, carer outcomes are only intermediate outcomes, part of the means to the end of client satisfaction and care, which are regarded as the final outcomes.

That there are clear conflicts of interest between carers and their dependants that put at odds the aims of maintaining care and increasing carer well-being, has been well demonstrated. Just how stark these conflicts of interest can be has been explored by, among others, Levin in her study of the supporters of elderly mentally infirm people. She found that the single greatest improvement in the mental health of such supporters came from the death or institutionalisation of their dependant (Levin et al., 1983). This is not to say, of course, that these supporters would necessarily have wished for such an institutionalisation. This point raises yet another complexity, which is the difference between people's wishes – and quite genuine wishes, not simply those they express publicly – and the consequences of situations for their well-being. People can and do choose to continue to do things that cause them considerable distress. Concentrating on the reduction of carer stress in isolation from wishes and values is therefore not effective.

This leads us to the third form of contradiction which relates to an issue of targeting. Should services be targeted on the most highly stressed carers or on those most liable to withdraw caregiving? As a number of studies have indicated, there is a relationship between stress and the likelihood of the withdrawal of the carer, but the relationship is not an exact one. Deciding that caregiving is more than one is able, or wishes, to manage can clearly occur at a number of levels of involvement. It may indeed be that the most crucial of such breaking points occur at the early stages, when few, or more likely no, service providers are involved. A policy targeted on the prevention of the marginal erosion of care may therefore find itself focusing resources on some very *lightly burdened*, and *relatively unstressed* carers, who are yet at this turning point.

There is, furthermore, some evidence from studies suggesting that male carers abandon caregiving at lower levels of both objective burden and subjectively experienced stress than do female carers (Levin et al., 1983; Wright, 1986). If this is indeed the case, a policy targeted on those on the margins will once again be predominantly focused on the less heavily burdened. It will, furthermore, raise major issues of equity and gender discrimination.

This brings us to a fourth area of tension which concerns the problems of generalisability. This is in a sense an extension of the previous issue concerning the aims of targeting.

If an agency targets on particular marginal situations, how can it explain the apparent breaches of equity involved in not providing help to other individuals who appear in terms of activity, burden, responsibility, even stress, to be in a similar situation? How can a public agency say that family X, who appear to be threatening to withdraw support, are to get services, but not family Y, who are in the same objective circumstances, but not expressing such a likelihood? What is the role in this, moreover, of 'manipulation' of the situation by the carer? How does one deal with the differential ability of different social groups to work the system?

There are parallels in this issue of generalisability with the problem of the costs of community care. Transferring people from institutions into the community appeared to be, if not cheaper, at least a comparable level of cost. But this is to a large extent a product of the inadequate provision of current services in the community whereby large numbers of comparably frail people receive little or no support. We cannot assume therefore that community care as a *whole* will be a cheaper or cost comparable option, since the implications of extending to *all* frail people currently living in the community, the levels of services that it is suggested are required for the support of those being deinstitutionalised, are very great indeed. So too, one can argue, would be the costs if one were to extend to all carers in the relevant category, the levels of support that have been suggested as a means to prevent breakdown in certain cases. Focusing on a particular outcome – deinstitutionalisation in the case of community care, or, here, the prevention of the marginal erosion of caregiving – can raise serious problems for a policy that has in fact much wider ramifications within social care generally.

Conclusions

In this paper I have tried to draw out some of the tensions in policy that relate to informal care. These, as I have suggested, have their roots in essentially conceptual problems, and they relate in major part to the ambiguous position occupied by carers within the social care system. As a result there is no single model of the relationship between agencies and informal carers; rather, a series of models or frames of reference are in operation. Concentrating on three of these – carers as resources, co-workers, co-clients – enables us to draw out in a schematic way some of the elements that underlie the current contradictions of policy in this field.

References

P. Abrams (1977), 'Community care: some research problems and priorities', *Policy and Politics*, 6:21, 125-151.

P. Abrams and M. Bulmer (1985), 'Policies to promote informal social care: some reflections on voluntary neighbourhood involvement and neighbourhood care', *Ageing and Society*, 5:1, 1-18.

G. Allen (1983), 'Informal networks of care: issues raised by Barclay', *British Journal of Social Work*, 13, 417-433.

Michael Bayley (1973), *Mental Handicap and Community Care*, Routledge, London.

Michael Bayley (1982), 'Helping care to happen in the city', in A. Walker (ed.), *Community Care: The Family, The State and Social Policy*, Blackwell, Oxford.

M. Bulmer (1987), *The Social Basis of Community Care*, Allen and Unwin, London.

M. Bulmer and P Abrams (1986), *Neighbours: The Work of Philip Abrams* Cambridge University Press, Cambridge.

G. Fennell, A.R. Emerson, M. Sidell and A. Hague (1981), *Day Centres for the Elderly in East Anglia*, Centre for East Anglian Studies, Norwich.

Janet Finch (1987), 'Whose responsibility? Women and the future of family care', in I. Allen, M. Wicks, J. Finch and D. Leat (eds.), *Informal Care Tomorrow*, Policy Studies Institute, London.

C. Froland (1981), 'Formal and informal care: discontinuities in a continuum', *Social Services Review*, 54.

C. Geertz (1973), *The Interpretation of Cultures*, Basic Books, New York.

C. Gilleard, E. Gilleard and J.E. Whittick (1984), 'Impact of psychogeriatric day hospital care on the patient's family', *British Journal of Psychiatry*, 145, 487-492.

E. Levin, I. Sinclair and P. Gorbach (1983), *The Supporters of Confused Elderly Persons at Home*, NISW, London.

R. Moroney (1976), *The Family and the State: Considerations for Social Policy*, Longman, London.

L. Rimmer and M. Wicks (1983), 'The challenge of change: demographic trends, the family and social policy', in H. Glennerster (ed.), *The Future of the Welfare State: Remaking Social Policy*, Heinemann, London.

J. Twigg (1988), '*Evaluation and the problems of its use in relation to support for informal carers*', Discussion Paper, Social

Policy Research Unit, York.

M. Wicks (1982), 'Community care and elderly people', in A. Walker (ed.), *Community Care: The Family, the State and Social Policy*, Blackwell, Oxford.

Fay D. Wright (1986), *Left to Care Alone*, Gower, Aldershot.

FURTHER READING

The following books and articles might be of additional help and interest to you. They are listed under relevant subject headings.

Psychology
This includes psychology of care and psychology of roles. You may wish to look at one or more of the following books for additional information related to psychology.

ORFORD, J. (1992) *Community Psychology: Theory and Practice,* John Wiley. This book contains a section on theory and a section on practice. The first section explores such issues as empowerment, social support in the community and particular problems in community psychology. The second section explores areas such as organisational psychology, self-help and illness prevention.

ROGERS, C. (1961) *On Becoming a Person: A therapist's view of psychology,* Houghton Mifflin, USA. This is a classic text which offers a humanistic approach to understanding ourselves and others.

Informal carers
The following book and articles are extremely useful (and readable) for exploring the issues surrounding the role and needs of informal carers.

GRANT, G. and NOLAN, M. (1993) 'Informal carers: sources and concomitants of satisfaction,' *Health and Social Care in the Community,* 1(3), pp. 147-51.

ROBINSON, K.M. (1993) 'Predictions of depression among informal caregivers,' *Nursing Research,* 30, pp. 359-63.

TWIGG, J. ed. (1992) *Carers: research and practice,* HMSO. This book has chapters by four contributing authors and explores issues surrounding numbers and types of carers and their similarities and differences, and roles of carers.

The mixed economy of care
Three publications are particularly useful as further reading on the mixed economy of care. These are:

GRIFFITHS, R. (1988) *Community Care: an agenda for action,* HMSO. This report led to the Community Care Act. It is in this report that the phrase 'mixed economy of care' was first used and defined.

HANDY, C. (1988) *Understanding Voluntary Organisations,* Penguin. This book explores the dynamics of voluntary work and voluntary organisations and the functions of voluntary groups.

LEAT, D. (1993) *The Development of Community Care by the Independent Sector,* Policy Studies Institute. This book explores the impact of the *Caring for people who live at home* initiative which was launched by the Department of Health in 1992. The aim of the initiative was to look at how the private and voluntary sectors could provide day and domiciliary services. Chapter 2 in particular explores the background and definitions of the mixed economy of care with regard to the role of the independent sector.

Transactional analysis
The following may be helpful in understanding this branch of psychology.

BERNE, E. (1964) *Games People Play*, Penguin. This is a classic book which explores the concept of 'games' in transactional analysis and how, through understanding games, we can understand our own behaviour and that of others.

JONGEWARD, D. and JAMES, H. (1984) *Winning Ways with People*, Addison Wesley. This is a workbook which applies transactional analysis to healthcare. It explains in understandable language the various concepts within transactional analysis.

REFERENCES

AGGLETON, P. (1991) *Health*, Routledge.

ALDRIDGE, J. and BECKER, S. (1993) 'Punishing the Children for Caring: the hidden cost of young carers', *Children and Society*, 7 (4): 376–87.

ALLAN, G. (1985) *Family life*, Blackwell.

ASTON, J. and SEYMOUR, D. (1990) *The New Public Health*, Open University Press.

ATKIN, K. (1992) 'Black Carers: the forgotten people', *Nursing the Elderly*, vol 4, no 2 :8–10.

ATKINSON, R.L., ATKINSON, C.A., SMITH, E.E., BEM, D.J. (1993) *Introduction to Psychology*, 11th Ed., Harcourt Brace, Jovanovich.

BALDWIN, S. (1993) *The Myth of Community Care: an alternative neighbourhood model of care*, Chapman & Hall.

BASS, D.M. and BOWMAN, K. (1990) 'Transition from Caregiving to Bereavement: the relationship of care related to strain and adjustment to death', *Gerontologist*, 31: 31–43.

BELBIN, R.M. (1981) *Management Teams*, Heinemann.

BELL, R., GIBBONS R. and PINCHEN, I. (1987) *Action Research with Informal Carers: patterns and processes in carers' lives*, Health Promotion Services.

BRAITHWAITE, V. A. (1990) *Bound to Care*, Allen & Unwin, Sydney.

BRODY, E.M. (1985) 'Parent Care as Normative Family Stress', *Gerontologist*, 21: 19–29.

BUNTING, S. (1989) 'Stress on Caregivers of the Elderly', *Advances in Nursing Science*, 11, pp. 176–96.

CLARKSON, S.E. *et al.* (1986) 'Impact of a handicapped child on mental health of parents', *British Medical Journal*, 293: pp. 1395–7.

CORBIN, J. and STRAUSS, A. (1988) 'Carers – working together', *Nursing Times*, 84 (15): 48–49.

DALLEY, G. (1988) *Ideologies of Caring: rethinking community and collectivism*, Macmillan.

DEPARTMENT OF HEALTH (1995) *Community Care Monitoring, NHS Executive and Report*, Health Publications Social Services Inspectorate.

DOUGLAS, R.L., HICKEY, T., NOEL, M. (1980) *Elder Abuse*, Ann Arbour: University of Michigan Press.

ELLERT, T. (1995) 'It couldn't be charity', *The Guardian* Society Section, 10 May :9.

FOUCAULT, M. (1972) *The Archaeology of Knowledge*, A. Sheridan, Tavistock.

GILHOOLY, M. (1986) 'Senile dementia: factors associated with caregiving preference for institutional care', *British Journal of Medical Psychology*, 59: 165–71.

GRAHAM, H. (1992) 'Community Care, Informal Care: problem or solution?' *Health Visitor*, 6 (12) : 444–5.

GRANT, G. and NOLAN, M. (1993) 'Informal carers: sources and concomitants of satisfaction', *Health and Social Care in the Community*, 1(3) : 147–51.

GREEN, H. (1988) *General Household Survey 1985: Informal Carers*, HMSO.

GRIFFITHS, R. (1988) *Community Care: an agenda for action*, HMSO.

GWYTHER, L.P. and GEORGE, L.K. (1986) 'Caregivers for Dementia Patients: complex determinants of well-being and burden', *Gerontologist*, 26 (3) : 245–7.

HANDY, C. (1988) *Understanding Voluntary Organisations*, Penguin.

HANDY, C. (1994) *The Empty Raincoat*, Hutchinson.

HEALTH SERVICES MANAGEMENT UNIT (1995) *Young Carers: an evaluation of three RHA projects in Merseyside*, HSMU, University of Manchester.

HIGGINS, J. (1989) 'Defining Community Care: realities and myths', *Social Policy and Administration*, Vol. 23, no.1 : 3–16.

HILLS, D. (1991) *Carer Support in the Community: evaluation of the Department of Health Initiative; Demonstration Districts for Informal Carers 1986–1989*, HMSO.

HOLLAND, J.L. (1973) *Making Vocational Choices*, New York, Prentice Hall.

HOOYMAN, N., GONYEA, J. and MONTGOMERY, R. (1985) 'The impact of in-home services termination on family caregivers', *Gerontologist* 24(2), :141–45.

JONES, L. (1994) *The Social Context of Health and Health Work*, Macmillan.

JONGEWARD, D. and JAMES, H. (1984) *Winning Ways with People*, Addison Wesley, California.

JOURARD, S.M. (1971) *The Transparent Self*, 2nd Ed. Van Nostrand, New York.

LAU, E. and KOSBERG, J. (1978) 'Abuse of the elderly by informal care providers', *Ageing*, Vol. 22, no. 9 : 5–10.

LEAT, D. (1993) *The Development of Community Care by the Independent Sector*, Policy Studies Institute.

LEVIN, E., SINCLAIR, I. and GORBACH, P. (1989) *Families, Services and Confusion in Old Age*, Gower.

LITTON, H. (1994) *The Irish Famine. An Illustrated History*, Wolfhound, Dublin.

MEANS, R. and SMITH, R. (1994) *Community Care: Policy and Practice*, Macmillan.

NOLAN, M.R., GRANT, G. and ELLIS, N.C. (1990) 'Stress in the eye of the beholder: reconceptualising the measurement of carer burden', *Journal of Advanced Nursing*, 15 :544–55.

PARKER, G. (1992) *With this Body: caring and disability in marriage*, Open University Press.

PARKER, G. and LAWTON, D. (1990) *Further Analysis of the 1985 General Household Survey Data on Informal Care. Report 1: A Typology of Caring*, Social Policy Research Unit.

QUINE, R. and PAHL, J. (1989) *Stress and coping in families caring for a child with severe mental handicap: A Longitudinal Study in Canterbury*, Institute of Social and Applied Services Studies, University of Kent.

ROBINSON, C. (1988) 'Learning to help: training for respite care', *Social Work Today*, 19:39.

ROBINSON, K. M. (1993) 'Predications of depression among informal caregivers', *Nursing Research*, 30: 59–63.

SANDWELL SOCIAL SERVICES DEPARTMENT (1989) *Caring for Carers Report: Child Carers Report Sandwell*, Sandwell Social Serevices Department.

SCOPE (1995) *Disabled in Britain: behind closed doors – the carers' experience*, SCOPE.

SILVERMAN, D. (1985) *Qualitative Methodology and Sociology*, Gower.

SOCIAL WORK SERVICES GROUP (1984) *Supporting the Informal Carers – fifty styles of caring: Models of practice for planner and practitioner*, Dept. of Health and Social Security.

SONTAG, S. (1983) *Illness as Metaphor*, Penguin.

THOMPSON, D. (1987) *Calling All Carers*, Association of Carers, South Manchester Branch.

TITMUSS, R. (1968) *Commitment to Welfare*, Allen & Unwin.

TWIGG, J. (1989) 'Models of Carers: how do social care agencies conceptualise their relationship with informal carers?', *Journal of Social Policy*, 18: 53–66.

TWIGG, J. (Ed) (1992) 'Carers in the Service System', *Carers: research and practice*, HMSO.

TWIGG, J. and ATKIN, K. (1993) *Policy and Practice in Informal Care*, Open University Press.

UNGERSON, C. (1987) *Policy is Personal: sex, gender and informal care*, Tavistock.

WHO (1987) 'The Ottowa Charter for Health Promotion', *Health Promotion*, 1 (4): iii-iv.

WILMOTT, P. and THOMAS, D. (1994) *Community in Social Policy*, Policy Studies Institute.

WOODHAM-SMITH, C. (1991) *Florence Nightingale*, Constable.

WRIGHT, F. D. (1986) *Left to Care Alone*, Gower.

GLOSSARY

Extended family–
the smallest family unit is known as the nuclear family. Units larger than the nuclear family are referred to as the extended family. This can include other family members such as grandparents or cousins.

Community care–
the current trend is for health services to be delivered as close to the patient as possible. This means that services previously delivered in hospital or in large institutional settings are now being delivered in the community. This does not always mean the home but can also include settings such as health centres, GPs' surgeries and local hospitals. It has also been extended to include day surgery where the procedure takes place in a hospital but the care and recovery occur at home.

Ministries–
Religious orders made up of and controlled by nuns or monks.

Mixed economy of care–
the provision of health and social services by a mix of agencies. The mix includes the statutory sector, the voluntary or non-governmental organisations (NGOs) and the private or business sector. Current governmental policy encourages the development of a mixed economy as it is claimed it provides more choice for users of services.

Purchasers–
in the reformed health and social services these are the people who buy health or social care on behalf of the public. In the health service these are the former district health authorities who have been reformed into purchasers or commissioners of services. They are responsible for buying health care for their resident populations. They incorporate a number of functions previously carried out by district health authorities and family health service authorities. The various local authorities are purchasers of social care.

Providers–
these are the various groups, institutions and statutory bodies which provide health and social services to individuals, groups and families. The current policy is to encourage a mix of service provision. This means that services traditionally delivered by the statutory sector no longer need necessarily be delivered in this manner. The voluntary and private sectors are now in a position to bid for and deliver these services. The main statutory providers in the health service are referred to as trusts.

Recognition–
is related to carers receiving due regard for professionalism, personal sacrifice and selflessness when performing their work. 'Reward' is related to financial payment or feelings of personal satisfaction resulting from the caring activity.

Ultra obligation–
Committing one's life to caring for another person.

PSYCHOLOGICAL ASPECTS OF CARING

in a mixed economy

Start date

Target completion date

Tutor for this topic

Contact number

USING THIS WORKBOOK

The workbook is divided into 'Sessions', covering specific subjects.

In the introduction to each learning pack there is a learner profile to help you assess your current knowledge of the subjects covered in each session.

Each session has clear learning objectives. They indicate what you will be able to achieve or learn by completing that session.

Each session has a summary to remind you of the key points of the subjects covered.

Each session contains text, diagrams and learning activities that relate to the stated objectives.

It is important to complete each activity, making your own notes and writing in answers in the space provided. **Remember this is your own workbook—you are allowed to write on it**.

Now try an example activity.

ACTIVITY

This activity shows you what happens when cells work without oxygen. This really is a physical activity, so please only try it if you are fully fit.

First, raise one arm straight up in the air above your head, and let the other hand rest by your side. Clench both fists tightly, and then open out your fingers wide. Repeat this at the rate of once or twice a second. Try to keep clenching both fists at the same rate. Keep going for about five minutes, and